Vintage Made Moder

Vintage
Made Modern

Transforming Timeworn Textiles into Treasured Heirlooms

✕✕✕✕✕✕✕✕✕✕✕✕✕

Jennifer Casa

✕✕✕✕✕✕✕✕✕✕✕✕✕

ROOST BOOKS

Boston & London

2014

Roost Books
An imprint of Shambhala Publications, Inc.
Horticultural Hall
300 Massachusetts Avenue
Boston, Massachusetts 02115
roostbooks.com

9 8 7 6 5 4 3 2 1

First Edition
Printed in China

♾ This edition is printed on acid-free paper that meets the
American National Standards Institute z39.48 Standard.
♻ Shambhala makes every effort to print on recycled paper.
For more information, please visit www.shambhala.com.

Distributed in the United States by Penguin Random House LLC
and in Canada by Random House of Canada Ltd

Designed by Lora Zorian

LIBRARY OF CONGRESS CATALOGING-IN-PUBLICATION DATA

Casa, Jennifer.
Vintage made modern: transforming timeworn textiles into
treasured heirlooms / Jennifer Casa.—First edition.
Pages   cm
ISBN 978-1-61180-123-1 (pbk.: alk. paper)
1. Clothing and dress—Remaking. 2. Sewing. 3. Vintage clothing.
4. Textile fabrics. 5. Recycling (Waste, etc.) 6. Textile crafts. I. Title.
TT550.C375 2014
646'.3—dc23
2013037241

Dedicated to my mom,
for sharing with me
her love of sewing,
patchwork
& quilting.

xoxo

Contents

*indicates a no-sew project

Introduction

They say love finds you when you least expect it. It found me one afternoon at an off-the-beaten-path antiques mall in the Amish countryside of northern Ohio. Peeking into a dusty chest of drawers, I discovered a gem—tucked away ever so carefully—in the form of a very old, unfinished patchwork quilt top made entirely of men's work shirts. It was a little piece of history that had been protected from the elements in that unassuming drawer for heaven knows how long.

I was immediately filled with wonder about the story behind this patchwork. I imagined a woman long ago—perhaps a mother like me—putting her time, love, and energy into each of those tiny, precise stitches, most likely over several seasons. What happened to the hands that once worked on this piece? Did some calamity occur that prevented them from continuing this beautiful handwork, or did life simply intervene, as it does for many of us, so the woman had to put this piece down, bringing the handwork to a halt? Whatever the reason, this piece of patchwork traveled through time and was right there in front of me: an unfinished object. This incomplete work-in-progress had likely been hibernating for generations. And, well, I could not in good conscience just leave it there.

So it began. A visit to that little shop on a dusty dirt road in the middle of nowhere awakened in me a passion for unfinished patchwork, cutter quilts, feed-sack prints, and vintage textiles of every kind. And my love of collecting these types of textiles has grown over the past many years. Something about surrounding myself with those fabrics is meditative—it reminds me of simpler times. Choices were few back then, not only because money was tight, but also because our world was smaller. Our ancestors were restricted to what was available to them locally, and yet what they created is extraordinary. In days when options were limited, one's creativity was stretched to span the spaces and places where materials were lacking. A fine example is the "make and mend" mentality of the early twentieth century; whether they were using charming prints available on grain sacks or leftover scraps from worn garments, imaginative makers utilized those bits to create artistic quilts, clothing, and home decor pieces that added beauty to a time that needed it. To be sure, we are fortunate to live in a modern world where most anything we can wish for is accessible and available—at a price, of course. I find that modern textiles can be exceptionally beautiful and inspiring (and hard to pass up!). The abundance of all that is new today, however, can also be overwhelming. With unlimited choices, it can be a challenge to make a decision and actually get down to the making. I suggest finding a balance in accumulating modern staples you tend to use frequently in your work (linen, solids, florals, etc.) and incorporating them with antique textiles that speak to you. Become a curator of your fabric stash, and create a happy marriage of vintage + modern in your work.

Perhaps you have found an amazing cutter quilt. Maybe an unfinished quilt top was handed down to you, and you do not quite know how to preserve it in a meaningful way. Or maybe, like me, you are an avid treasure hunter who cannot say no to well-loved linens. We all appreciate the handcrafted value in these pieces, but oftentimes, due to wear and tear, we cannot use them as originally intended. This book will take you by the hand and guide you through projects that preserve and showcase these wonderful materials in a modern context. We will honor the handwork that went into a variety of vintage finds, and respectfully repurpose these treasured textiles, transforming them into modern heirlooms.

Truth be told, when I bought that first quilt top, I honestly could not see myself restoring it as a proper quilt. A project of that size was not in my skill set at the time, nor was I particularly interested in finishing what someone else had started. I did, however, have a clear vision for that beautiful piece of unfinished patchwork, one that I hoped would do it justice and enable it to become more than it had been when I first discovered it. Seam ripper in hand, I carefully released some of the stitching to free a long chain of patches, and used the chain to create a one-of-a-kind wreath for our front door. And that lovely wreath was just the beginning. I was able to share the beautiful handwork and history of that single quilt top in the form of more wreaths, notebook covers, pencil

pouches, handbags, pillows, and so much more. True, I followed a different path than was the original maker's intention for this quilt top; but the enjoyment of that single piece blossomed exponentially because her work is now showcased in functional, modern heirlooms. Our collaboration transcends time; her work from generations ago is now connected with mine, our stitches intertwined and enjoyed by many. I sincerely hope I did the maker proud.

My mother is a quilter. When I was in junior high school, she brought me along to the fabric store to select the prints for what would one day become my quilt. Then she spent the next twelve years (yes, twelve!) lovingly piecing the twenty sampler squares that make up my quilt. Slowly but surely, stitch after hand-quilted stitch, she made progress. Years after having completed college and graduate school, I found myself back home to visit, after having spent the summer in Germany preparing for another year of teaching. I was sleeping off jet lag and awoke to find my quilt tucked around me on the bed. It was finished! No words can describe what went into this quilt, all the ups and downs of life that transpired during the many years she spent stitching—it is all in there. I have a great respect for the time, love, and effort that go into this type of handwork. Having made several quilts myself, I know that the process is very meditative and the maker's heart and soul are in the stitches. A quilt is more than a quilt; it is a snapshot of everything and everyone connected to it. It is history.

Someday, long after I am gone, my quilt may also lose its way in the shuffle of life. If it does, perhaps it will come into the hands of someone who sees potential in its timeworn, well-loved stitches. Perhaps someone will take it home and allow it to continue being appreciated and used in a meaningful way that respects the history in each and every stitch. I embrace everything that went into my quilt, all that it has been and continues to be at this moment; and I am charmed to imagine what is yet to come.

Every pretty, old thing has a tale to tell. Making pretty things from vintage treasures is a way to write yet another chapter in stories composed long ago, with you becoming part of the narrative.

Step into my time machine. Let's make something special. xoxo

Working with Timeworn Textiles

Throughout this book, you will be recycling just as generations before us have, utilizing timeworn textiles with histories of their own. Just because these materials are ripped or stained does not negate their value. On the contrary, these are pieces that deserve recognition and appreciation. With a little resourcefulness, gentle care, and some creative repurposing, you can breathe life back into these textiles, refresh their beauty, and create new memories of your own.

Sourcing

For as long as I can remember, I have enjoyed popping into thrift stores and off-the-beaten-path antiques malls to see what treasures I might find. In recent years, my children are almost always along for the ride. What a joy to have two eager little treasure hunters in my company! We enjoy ourselves as we wander, imagine, and make discoveries—there is so much to see; you just have to know where to look. As anyone who thrifts regularly knows, there are especially good days to stop into your favorite spots—some shops add new stock only at specific increments, while others may feature terrific sale days. But, honestly, you never know what you will find on any given day. And that is part of the fun.

The best way to find textile treasures is to go look for them. Make a regular date to pop into your local thrift shops and say hello. (And, while you are at it, bring along a bag of clothes/toys/housewares to donate.) If you find yourself with a few free hours, create your very own treasure map of nearby estate and garage sales. Wander the aisles of antiques

fairs and rummage sales, and peruse the abundance of online sources for vintage textiles, as well. There is so much inspiration out there, and temptations abound for even the most disciplined shoppers. We do so love pretty, vintage things, and a few bits always seem to find their way home with us. I simply cannot let them sit and gather dust any longer.

When you come across vintage quilts, patchwork, and linens, give them a thorough once over to determine if they possess the qualities you are looking for, and carefully consider your endgame. Are you planning to use the piece as is? Might you consider having professionals restore it? Or do you have repurposing in mind? When it comes to repurposing vintage textiles, I encourage you to make use of the truly worn and tattered ones, salvaging their usable bits to be transformed into new creations. It is a great way to extend the life of these cherished textiles, and the possibilities are endless.

Care

Typically, once we arrive home with our textile treasures, I inspect each one more closely for damage such as stains and tears, and then I remove any pins and tags from the point of sale. Antique and vintage textiles—especially the tattered ones—require gentle care

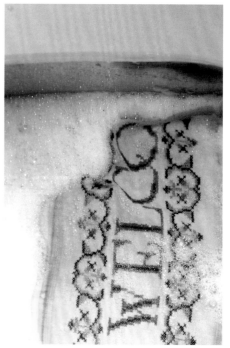

and cleaning to maintain and sustain them. If you wish to have an old quilt repaired or restored, consider contacting a professional textile conservator before attempting to fix it yourself. If, however, your pieces have more sentimental value, and you wish to continue using them (such as a family quilt), you can patch up the threadbare spots with pieces of complementary vintage fabrics. Even if your materials are earmarked for repurposing, when they come into your hands, you will likely first need to clean up and care for your pretty, old things.

If something is particularly dusty or musty, you can lay a piece of thin mesh or screening over it, and then use a vacuum hose to remove excess dirt and dust without disturbing the delicate fibers of the piece. To wash vintage textiles, place your pieces in mesh bags for a nice cold-water bath in the washer on a delicate cycle with a gentle de-tergent. If, however, you think that machine washing may damage the fabrics, then wash them by hand in the sink or bathtub. There are special vintage textile soaks available for these delicate fabrics, or you can use a tiny bit of baby shampoo. (Some say that a gentle denture cleaner is useful in removing stains and brightening fabrics, too.) After your pieces have had a long soak in cool water and a delicate wash, rinse them well. To dry, first lay your piece flat on a towel and roll it up to gently extract excess water, and then allow it to dry on a towel, drying rack, or the line if you think the textile can handle sunlight. (Many people discourage machine-drying vintage fabrics; however, I confess to having done it many times with what I would consider to be sturdy pieces, and every-thing turned out fine.) Use your best judgment when cleaning and caring for your fab-rics. After all, you want them to continue to be well loved, long into the future.

Once the pieces are dry, you will want to be mindful of storing them appropriately. Remember that natural cotton and linen fibers need to breathe, and storing them away from dust and direct sunlight is best—a cabinet with glass doors would be perfect and would also allow you to enjoy the aesthetics of your treasured fabric stash when not in use. Wool, on the other hand, is best kept airtight because this is its only true defense against pests—tuck some lavender Sweet Sachets (page 48) in with your woolens as fur-ther protection to ward off pesky moths. Proper cleaning and care of your materials will promote their sustainability for generations to come.

Repurposing

Once you've washed your textiles and they are ready to be used, consider what went into the creation of quilts, patchwork, and other handmade materials when choosing new uses for them. That being said, under most circumstances, you should not feel obligated to finish someone else's work, or feel limited to use any given piece as is. I encourage you to honor and showcase original handwork in your home, as well as in your creations, and make the most of your materials.

"Timeworn" textiles are pieces that cannot be used as originally intended without major grafting. Bits can be salvaged, but the piece as a whole is beyond repair by even the most talented seamstress. I love those threadbare bits just as much as the prettiest little feed-sack squares in mint condition. Being mindful to use tattered, unfinished, or unusable textiles in their current state is a thoughtful way to repurpose materials that otherwise would have been overlooked. It is a considerate way of extending their life, creating many new pieces from something that might have gone sadly unused. The artisanship is awe-inspiring, and the fabrics—oh the fabrics!—let them do the talking. It is so lovely when vintage fabrics are able to take center stage in new formats, allowing you to swoon over the intricate handwork and think about the journey they have traveled, ultimately bringing them to you in the here and now.

The projects in this book provide you with simple instructions to salvage and deconstruct a variety of timeworn textiles for practical use, with as little waste as possible. I encourage you to swap out one textile for another in any of the projects, mix and match designs, and use inspiration to make them your own. And, by all means, save your scraps for later use! Repurposing in this way renews the essence of your treasured vintage textiles as modern pieces that will be further enjoyed for years to come. It is an opportunity for you to travel through time, become a historian, and collaborate with generations past in the creation of one-of-a-kind pieces to be used now and held dear long into the future. You will make something special, indeed!

Simple Sewing Tool Kit

The projects presented in this book assume a basic knowledge of sewing and do not require special skills; in fact, some projects involve no sewing at all. Whether you intend to follow a particular project as written, or make adjustments to suit your fancy, it is a good idea to get the lay of the land and read through the instructions prior to getting started. When working with vintage fabrics, you will want to be especially careful, of course, because most are irreplaceable. Take your time, plan your projects, and use plenty of pins to secure bits and pieces prior to firing up your sewing machine. Here is a quick reference for the sewing tools used in projects throughout this book.

Hoops (Quilt + Embroidery)

Use hoops to hold your quilt or foundation piece(s) taut for even hand-stitching.

Needles

Hand-sewing needles are available in many sizes. (If you can find vintage needle books with new needles inside, try using those needles when hand-sewing delicate vintage fabrics.)

Quilting needles have a sharp, tapered tip designed to go through the many layers of a quilt.

Embroidery needles are slightly thicker with a wide eye and a light ballpoint.

Universal sewing-machine needles are available in various sizes and sharpness for different uses. (I recommend keeping on hand a few assortment packs of universal sewing-machine needles; these include several sizes to accommodate various thicknesses of fabrics.)

Straight Pins

Fine, sharp pins are essential to keep fabrics positioned precisely for sewing delicate textiles.

Quilter's Ruler

This clear, plastic piece has a ruled grid especially helpful for precise measuring, marking, and cutting.

Rotary Cutter + Self-Healing Cutting Mat

This combo makes cutting a breeze and is incredibly useful for cutting fabric into everything from strips to curves to larger pieces.

Scissors

Have a few scissors on hand that are dedicated to specific uses—large scissors for cutting fabric, small scissors beside your machine for snipping threads, retractable travel scissors to keep in your handwork basket, and so on—and label each one.

Seam Ripper

This sharp little tool is useful for getting into tight stitches to undo patchwork (or mistakes, *ahem*) without wasting a bit of fabric. As you can imagine, it is many sewers' best friend!

Sewing Machine

Whether your sewing machine is as basic as it comes or fully computerized with hundreds of stitches and presser feet, as long as you know your way around your machine, you are good to go!

Be sure to keep your machine's user manual nearby for quick reference, too.

Threads

A wide variety of cotton, polyester, silk, and other threads are specifically designed for use with quilting, embroidery, hand-sewing, and so forth, readily available at craft and sewing stores.

Walking Foot

This presser foot is especially useful for machine quilting and when working with thick fabrics. It functions by synchronizing the top feed of layered fabrics through the machine in conjunction with the lower feed dogs, and it keeps the many layers from shifting.

Water-Soluble Pens

The ink in these pens disappears with a simple spritz of water, making them a great tool for marking directly on fabrics for embroidery, quilting, and more.

Your Imagination

By far, your imagination is the most essential element of all! Be brave, try, try again, and have fun!

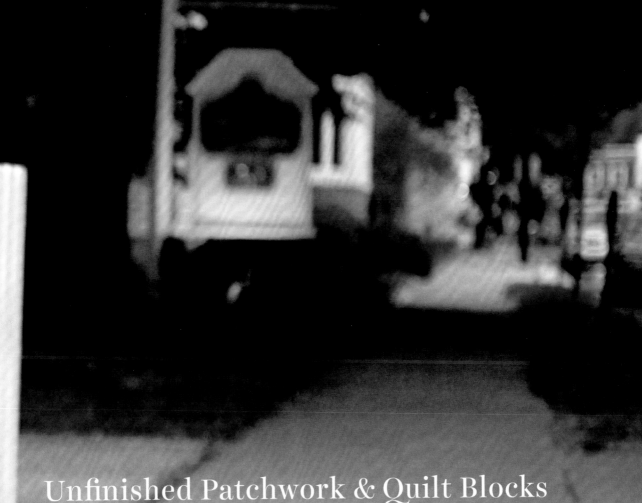

Unfinished Patchwork & Quilt Blocks

Unfinished patchwork and quilt blocks are the stuff of pure magic: simply touch the stitches, and you enter history. Abandoned works-in-progress like these present you with the unique opportunity for a collaboration that transcends time. Imagine your handwork joined with that from generations ago, your stitches intertwined with those of makers past. Quilt tops and large-scale pieces (as well as the tiniest remnants and scraps) are out there, waiting to become something special... waiting for you.

What will you make?

Grandmother's Hexagon Hot Pad

Grandmother's Flower Garden is one of the most popular quilt patterns of all times, featuring an intricate mosaic of hexagons. Lovely, oh, yes! But the labor-intensive nature of hand-piecing this honeycomb pattern often kept many of these quilts from ever being completed. As a result, beautiful vintage remnants are easy to find when treasure hunting. They present you with an opportunity to reinterpret a classic in a modern context. I love using simple appliqué to accentuate their shape, as well as to showcase all their lovely fabrics in these thick felt trivets.

FINISHED MEASUREMENTS

Projects shown are a 9" square and a 12" diameter hexagon cutout. (But you can make whatever size you like.)

WHAT YOU NEED

- One fully pieced hexagon flower (about 8" in diameter, or any size you wish)
- 3 mm thick wool felt: (1 square) 1"–2" larger than the diameter of your hexagon flower
- Walking foot for your sewing machine (optional, but very helpful)
- Embroidery floss (optional)

HOW TO MAKE

Note: Backstitch beginning and end of each line of stitches.

1. Center the hexagon flower with the right side facing up on the wool felt square. Pin in place.
2. Machine appliqué (or hand-sew) the hexagon flower directly to the felt by stitching first around the perimeter of the center hexagon, then around the perimeter of the next layer of hexagons, and finally around the perimeter of the outer layer of hexagons.
3. Use embroidery floss to add a border of blanket stitching around the entire edge of the square for an old-fashioned look, or use sharp scissors to cut a border ¼" larger than the outer edge of each hexagon to highlight the unique shape.

Mini-Project: Hexagon Flower Appliqué

Unfinished patchwork pieces, in particular these hexagon flowers, lend themselves quite well to appliqué. Here are two of my favorite ways to use them:

HEXAGON FLOWER JOURNAL PAIRS

I particularly like to feature the geometric design of hexagon flowers on kraft-paper notebooks—you halve a hexagon flower for use in creating two sweet journals: one to keep and one to share.

To Make: Simply use a glue stick to adhere half of a hexagon flower to the cover of a Moleskine or similar journal, aligning the straightedge with the open edge of the notebook. Then topstitch around the entire piece, just inside the edge to secure the fabric directly to the journal cover. (Note: Your needle will dull from sewing through paper, so be sure to switch to a fresh one for your next fabric project.)

HEXAGON FLOWER PATCH

Consider also that your favorite vintage patchwork bits are a wonderful medium to use in your mending. A hexagon flower added to my daughter's skirt cleverly masks an unsightly tear and creates a lovely decorative element.

To Make: Apply paper-backed fusible web (such as Wonder Under or HeatnBond) to the back of your patchwork according to the manufacturer's directions. When cooled, remove the paper backing and place the patchwork over the area in need of mending, and then adhere it to the fabric according to the manufacturer's directions. Finish by topstitching the perimeter of the hexagon flower directly onto your piece.

Ever wondered how those sweet hexagons are made so precisely? Well, the process is actually simpler than you may think. These hexagons come together rather quickly, and are a terrific way to showcase your favorite vintage fabric scraps. They are also an ideal handwork project to take along with you to all the sidelines and waiting rooms in your life. Refer to the Stitch Guide (page 123) for a step-by-step tutorial, and learn how to make your own.

Dresden Doll

Colorful quilts added much-needed cheer to many American homes during the Great Depression of the 1930s. A very popular pattern of the time was the Dresden Plate, which featured pie-shaped scraps of pretty fabrics hand-stitched in a circle, then appliquéd to a foundation piece. These blocks were lovingly made, over and over again, and set aside in stacks until there were enough to create an entire quilt. You will often find this beautiful patchwork in varying stages of completion, each with slivers of oh-so-pretty fabrics, every one more charming than the next. Over the years, I have collected my fair share of these treasures, setting them aside for "someday" when I would figure out what to make of them. And then, one day, I noticed how the patchwork arc resembles the lines of a simple dress, and I transformed this shapely patchwork into soft, mini-me dolls for my girls.

FINISHED MEASUREMENTS

Approximately 13" from head to toe

WHAT YOU NEED

- Dresden Plate patchwork block with pie-shaped wedges that taper from at least 1½" at the narrow end to 3½" at the wider end, and measuring about 5" in length
- Linen fabric for the limbs: (1 piece) 5" × 10"
- Linen fabric for the face: (1 piece) 4½" circle
- Fabric in desired hair color: (1 piece) 4½" circle for the back of head and scraps for the face
- Wool stuffing or poly-fill
- Walking foot for your sewing machine (optional, but very helpful)
- Embroidery floss

HOW TO MAKE

Note: Backstitch beginning and end of each line of stitches.

1. Use a seam ripper to deconstruct 2 pieces, each with 3 connected wedges (for the dress) from the patchwork. Cut out 1 additional wedge (to be used for the shoes), and then trim the shoe fabric to an even rectangle measuring 1½" wide × 5" long.

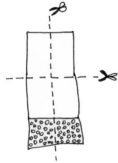

2. Align one long edge of the shoe fabric (right sides together) with the short end of linen for the limbs. Pin in place. Using a ¼" seam allowance, sew the fabrics together. Press the seam to one side on the wrong side, and then press again on the right side.

3. Cut a 5" square off the linen end, and then cut that piece in half (to become the arms). Cut the linen with the shoe fabric in half vertically to be used to create legs and shoes.

4. Fold each of the four fabric rectangles for the limbs in half lengthwise, with right sides together. For the arms, sew the long side and one short side closed. For the legs, sew the long side and the short end with the shoe fabric closed. Clip the corners, and then press on both sides.

5. Use a chopstick, bone folder, or the end of a paintbrush to turn the limbs right side out.

6. Fill both the arms and legs with stuffing, leaving about 1" unstuffed. Set aside.

7. Using a ⅛" seam allowance, topstitch the fabric scraps on the linen fabric for the face to represent bangs and other features. Turn the face over, and trim any fabric extending beyond the circular shape of the linen.

8. Place the linen face piece on top of the front dress with right sides facing, and pin in place where the chin meets the neck. Sew together along the neck using a ¼" seam allowance. Press the seam to one side on the wrong side, and then press again on the right side. Repeat for the other dress piece and back of the head.

9. Pin the legs to the right of the front hemline about ⅓ of the way in from either corner with feet pointing up toward the neck, and then sew the legs to the dress using a ¼" seam allowance. Pin the arms to the right side of the dress sides, about 1" down from the neck seam as if the arms are crossing the chest; sew the arms to the dress using a ¼" seam allowance.

10. With the legs pointed up and the arms folded closed, pin the doll front to the doll back with its right sides together. Using a ¼" seam allowance, sew around the entire doll, being careful to line up the seams at the neck and along the dress. Leave a 3" area open for turning along a bottom edge of the dress.

11. Carefully turn the doll right side out through the opening, and then gently push into the head and corners with a chopstick. Fill the doll head and dress with stuffing. Blind stitch the opening closed by hand. Give it a few squeezes to distribute the stuffing evenly throughout the doll.

12. Hand-stitch desired features on the doll's face using embroidery floss.

Would you like to make a Dresden Plate block using fabrics of your own choosing? Refer to the Stitch Guide (page 122) for a step-by-step tutorial, and learn how to make one for yourself.

Decoupatchwork Gallery Frame

It is hard to resist all the pretty fabrics in old patchwork. Each tiny piece is a treasure in and of itself. This project is a great way to use up your favorite vintage fabric scraps from tattered or stained quilt tops. Use a seam ripper to liberate the prettiest squares, and showcase them in a special frame that is a work of art on its own.

FINISHED MEASUREMENTS

Project shown 14" × 14" (But you could make whatever size you like.)

WHAT YOU NEED

- Scraps of your favorite vintage fabrics (I like to use 4" or larger strips and squares.)
- Wooden picture frame or four artist's stretcher bars assembled as a frame
- A small paintbrush
- Wax paper
- Decoupage medium (such as Mod Podge)
- Sawtooth picture hanger (if needed)

HOW TO MAKE

1. Place a piece of wax paper on your work surface to protect it from the adhesive.
2. Paint a layer of decoupage medium onto a small area of the front of the frame.
3. Place a fabric piece directly on top of the adhesive, and smooth out any bubbles with your fingertips. Apply more adhesive to adhere the fabric to the frame completely, wrapping it around to the back of the frame.
4. Paint another thin layer of decoupage medium directly on top of the fabric to seal it.
5. Continue to apply your fabrics one at a time in this manner, overlapping the edges slightly as you adhere each first to the front of the frame then wrap it over to the back.
6. Allow to dry completely, and then apply an additional coat of decoupage medium to the entire piece.
7. If needed, attach a picture hanger to the back of the frame for display purposes.

Mix Match Note-Taker

No matter how many innovative gadgets are available to help us get organized, I find nothing is better than good old-fashioned paper and pencil. And when you combine them with some of your favorite vintage fabric bits, you end up with a handy catchall for your to-dos and whatnots. I like to think of these note-takers as short-term memory insurance wrapped up in pretty patchwork.

FINISHED MEASUREMENTS

4¼" × 6½" (closed), 8⅝" × 6" (open)

WHAT YOU NEED

- Vintage patchwork for the exterior: (1 piece) 9⅝" × 7½"
- Cotton batting: (1 piece) 9⅝" × 7½"
- Muslin or plain cotton fabric: (1 piece) 9⅝" × 7½"
- Linen or cotton fabric for the lining: (2 pieces) 9⅝" × 7½"
- 8" piece of thin bias tape or ribbon, string, yarn, or twine for the tie
- Water-soluble marking pen (or chalk)
- 1 complementary vintage button
- 3" × 5" index cards or scrap paper
- Pencil or pen
- Walking foot for your sewing machine (optional, but very helpful)

HOW TO MAKE

Note: Backstitch beginning and end of each line of stitches.

1. Create a quilt sandwich with the muslin on the bottom, batting in the middle, and exterior patchwork piece right side up on top. Pin this sandwich together to keep the fabric from shifting while quilting.
2. Machine or hand quilt the sandwich. (I am fond of using a few different colored threads to stitch bunches of lines both vertically and horizontally, but you are free to quilt your sandwich in any manner you like.) Press with an iron when done.
3. Fold one of the lining pieces lengthwise, with the right side facing out. Press

on the fold, and then topstitch along the fold using a ⅛" seam allowance. Press along the fold once again. This will become the pocket piece.

4. Position the quilt sandwich right side up so that it is wider than it is tall. Center the ribbon on top of it, running sideways so that it extends about 1" beyond one side and rests at least 1" inward from the other side. Next, place the pocket piece on top, aligning the raw edge along the bottom. Finally, place the second piece of lining fabric right side down on top of everything. Pin the entire piece together, including where the ribbon is positioned. Using a ⅜" seam allowance, sew together around all four sides, leaving a 3" opening for turning. Press on both sides.

5. Clip the corners, and then carefully turn the piece right side out through the opening. Gently press into the corners with your finger or a chopstick, being careful not to poke through the stitching. Press well on both sides, and pin the opening closed.

6. Using a ¼" seam allowance, topstitch around the entire piece—while doing this step, you will secure the opening. Run a few extra stitches over the section with the ribbon. Topstitch again using a ⅛" seam allowance.

7. Place the piece so that the lining is facing up. Fold in half, and finger crease the spine. With the lining and pocket facing, use a water-soluble pen or chalk to mark two lines, each ½" to either side of the center crease. Topstitch along both lines to secure the pocket to the rest of the piece. Press on both sides.

8. Fold the piece closed to determine placement for the button on the front, using the ribbon as a guide. Stitch the button in place by hand.

9. Insert blank index cards or scrap paper into one of the pockets, and place a pencil in the center sleeve. Use the other pocket to organize your active notes, corral your receipts, or simply stash meaningful bits that make you happy.

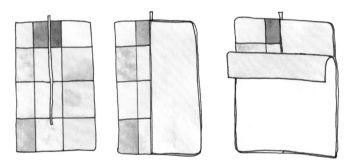

Feed-Sack Charm Pendant

Creative farm women in the 1800s repurposed the fabrics from printed grain sacks to make everything from home goods to clothing and—you guessed it—quilts. Feed sacks featured prints that were so very endearing that parting with even the tiniest scrap was hard. These charms are a wonderful way to showcase the beauty in even the smallest remnants of salvaged feed-sack fabrics.

FINISHED MEASUREMENTS

1" circle

WHAT YOU NEED

- 1" or larger scraps of your favorite feed-sack or similar small-scale print fabrics
- 1" wooden discs, approximately ¼" thick (found at craft stores)
- Scissors
- A small paintbrush
- Wax paper
- Matte decoupage medium (such as Mod Podge)
- Hand drill with ⅛" bit
- Fine-grit sandpaper or a rough-edged fingernail file
- Thin leather or hemp cording for stranding your necklace
- Plaid Brand Dimensional Magic (optional)

HOW TO MAKE

1. Trace your wooden shapes onto the fabric scraps, and cut out the shapes.
2. Place a piece of wax paper on your work surface to protect it from the adhesive.
3. Paint a thin layer of decoupage medium onto one side of a wooden disc. Place a fabric piece directly on top of the wooden disc, and smooth out any bubbles with your fingertip.
4. Paint another thin layer of decoupage medium directly on top of the fabric to seal it to the disc. Set aside and allow a few minutes to dry. Make as many as you like, and by the time you've finished the last one, the first one will most likely be dry and ready for the next step.

5. Use a hand drill to make a small hole about ¼" in from the edge of each disc.

6. Smooth off any rough edges of each disc and around the drilled holes with fine-grit sandpaper or a fingernail file.

7. Place each of the discs fabric side up onto the wax paper, and apply a second coat of decoupage medium to seal it, or apply a layer of Dimensional Magic (which creates a thick glossy top coat for a lovely finish). Allow it to dry according to the manufacturer's instructions.

8. Cut a length of cording that is a few inches longer than the circumference of your head. (You want to be sure you can get the necklace on and off easily.)

9. Holding the two cut ends together, feed them from the front to back through the hole in the charm and then through the loop created in the cord. Pull to secure the knot at the top of the charm. Knot the ends to wear.

Mini-Project: Charming Buttons and Bracelets

These little fabric charms are each so sweet and unique, and it is fun to think up new ways to wear them. Here are a few ideas you might like.

CHARMING BUTTONS

Another fun use for these charms is as buttons for cardigans and shirts, as accessories, or simply as sewn-on decoration.

To Make: Create the charms as for the pendants, but drill two or four holes in each charm. Smooth the edges as before, and apply Dimensional Magic to the surface of each button (being careful not to get it into the holes). Allow to dry overnight, and then stitch the buttons onto any garment you wish to infuse with a bit of feed-sack charm.

BRACELET CHARMS

String up a few of your favorite buttons or charms as simple friendship bracelets to share with your friends.

To Make: Work half your desired length of any friendship bracelet pattern before incorporating a charm into the weaving. Then lace the embroidery floss through a charm or button and pull tightly to secure it to the bracelet before continuing to weave according to your chosen pattern.

Cutter Quilts

You have no doubt seen cutter quilts gathering dust in flea markets, antiques shops, garage sales, and the like—these dear old quilts are well-loved pieces of history. They have lived a good life for a quilt, but some have become so tattered, threadbare, and stained that they are no longer usable as originally intended. Do not be put off by their imperfections, however, for that is also part of their story.

Now take a closer look. Note the beauty in those antique fabrics, and ponder the potential in their timeworn, well-loved stitches. Cutter quilts present you with an opportunity to combine your efforts with those from generations past. You can make it possible for something special to continue being appreciated and used in a meaningful way that honors the history in every stitch. Help these quilts find a new purpose.

Be creative. Be inspired. Be respectful. Become part of their story.

Sweet Sachets

These charming scented bags are perfect to tuck in among your unmentionables, or to freshen up your luggage, your car, or even your desk. I like to make many of these in one sitting and let the children stash them in drawers throughout the house. Using cutter quilt pieces for these sachets gives them a pillowlike charm that is further enhanced by the soothing aroma of dried lavender. An added benefit of dried lavender is that it naturally wards off moths and insects. Quality dried lavender buds should maintain their fragrance for at least a year; when you notice the aroma beginning to fade, you can refresh the sachets by gently crushing them in your palm. Consider also using other dried aromatics, including chamomile, cloves and cinnamon, winter savory, rosemary, and cedar chips.

FINISHED MEASUREMENTS
About 3" × 3"

WHAT YOU NEED

- Cutter quilt scraps: (2 pieces) 4" × 4"
- Walking foot for your sewing machine (optional, but very helpful)
- Dried lavender buds (about ½ cup)

HOW TO MAKE

Note: Backstitch beginning and end of each line of stitches.

1. Pin the cutter quilt squares right sides together. Stitch the squares together around the perimeter using a ½" seam allowance, leaving one side open for turning and filling.
2. Clip the corners, and then press on both sides. Turn the sachet right side out, and press again.
3. Fill the sachet ¾ full with dried lavender.
4. On the open side, fold the raw edges under ½" and stitch the opening closed by hand. Topstitch the entire piece using a ¼" seam allowance, if desired.

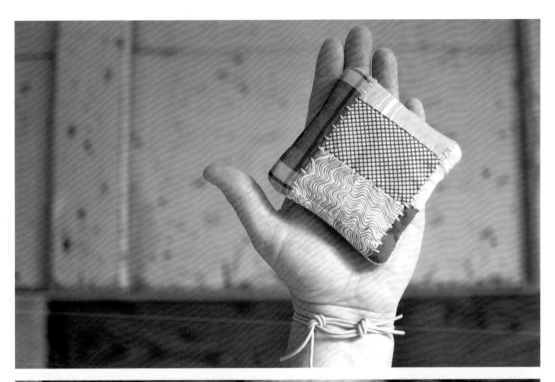

Mini-Project: Reusable Hand Warmers

There are so many alternative uses for these sweet quilted sachets, and one of my favorites is as reusable hand warmers. How cozy you will feel when you tuck a few of these in your pockets on a cold winter's day! Not to mention how charming they are when made from bits of antique quilts.

To Make: Create the sachets as written using cutter quilt pieces, filling them with uncooked rice instead of dried herbs. If you like, add a few drops of essential oils for fragrance. Sew the opening closed, as with the lavender sachets. When you wish to warm them up, simply microwave the hand warmers for 15 seconds prior to use and then place into your coat pockets.

Häuschen Doorstop

When the weather is nice and fresh air breezes through your home, stand this simple little house (Häuschen) against your open door to stop it from blowing shut. Functional, to be sure, but it is also a way to showcase your favorite cutter quilt with just a touch of whimsy. The patchwork mimics bricks or siding, and simple embroidery on the linen roof echoes the lines of traditional slate tiles. And it is a far prettier alternative than most hardware doorstops.

FINISHED MEASUREMENTS

A pleasingly plump 8" wide × 5" deep × 9" high

WHAT YOU NEED

- Cutter quilt piece for the house base: (1 piece) 28" × 5½"
- Cutter quilt piece for the house bottom: (1 piece) 8" × 5½"
- Linen fabric for the roof front and back: (2 pieces) 7" × 9"
- Linen fabric for the roof sides: (1 piece) 12" × 6"
- Häuschen Roof Side pattern piece (found in the Resources section of this book)
- Walking foot for your sewing machine (optional, but very helpful)
- 2 pounds of dried beans
- Wool stuffing or poly-fill
- Embroidery floss

HOW TO MAKE

Note: Backstitch beginning and end of each line of stitches.

1. Fold the large cutter quilt piece in half, right sides together, aligning the two short ends. Using a ½" seam allowance, sew the short edges together. Press the seam open on the wrong side, and then press again on the right side.

2. Pin the house bottom piece to the house base with right sides together. Start by aligning the base seam with the center of one of the 8" sides of the bottom piece, and then pin around all four sides. Using a ½" seam allowance, sew the bottom to the base.

3. Now for the roof. Place the two pieces of fabric for the roof front and back right sides together, and pin in place along one of the 9" sides. Using a ¼" seam allowance, sew that 9" side together leaving a 3" opening in the middle for turning later. Press the seam open on the wrong side, then again on the right side.

4. Use the pattern piece to cut out two roof sides from the linen fabric. Pin one of the triangular roof sides to the roof with right sides together, aligning the 6" sides of the triangle along the roof front and back; make sure the top corner of the triangle meets at the seam where the roof front and back join. Using a ¼" seam allowance, sew the edges together, being careful when turning at the join. Repeat for the other roof side piece. Press all seams on both sides.

5. With the house inside out, place the roof upside down inside the house base so that their right sides are together. Pin together around the entire edge where the base meets the roof. Using a ½" seam allowance, sew the base and the roof together.

6. Reach inside the house through the opening in the roof to turn the house right side out. Gently press into the corners with your finger.

7. Fill the base with two pounds of dried beans, and then add stuffing until you have a full little house. Hand-stitch the opening closed using a blind stitch.

8. Embroider tiles onto the linen to simulate a slate roof.

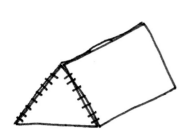
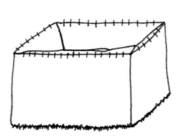

Aunt Betty's Bangles

These soft, chunky bangle bracelets will add a nice bit of vintage/modern style to your wardrobe. Slip a stack over your wrist to dress up whatever you are wearing, be it your favorite summer dress or jeans and a T-shirt. The contrast of your favorite charming fabrics with a classic bangle shape will make them a treasured go-to accessory.

FINISHED MEASUREMENTS

Projects shown are 8½" around with varying widths

WHAT YOU NEED

- Cutter quilt scraps
- ½" wide ribbon
- Fabric glue (such as Fabri-Tac)
- Thread in a complementary color for your bobbin (optional)

HOW TO MAKE

1. First, make your bangle pattern piece. Hold out your hand is if you were going to slip on a bangle bracelet, and measure comfortably around the widest part of your hand to determine the length for your pattern. Determine the desired width of your bangles, and double that number for your pattern piece. For example, if you would like a bangle that is 2" wide, your pattern piece will be 4" wide × the circumference of your hand. Sketch your bangle pattern onto a piece of paper, and cut it out.

2. Use your pattern piece to measure and cut out fabric from a cutter quilt for your bracelet.

3. Fold your fabric in half with the wrong sides together, and press to create a center crease lengthwise. Open the piece up, and position it on your work surface with the right side facing down. Fold one long edge toward that center crease so that the right side is facing you, and press. Repeat for the other long side, and press again on both sides.

4. Cut a piece of ribbon that measures the length of your bangle. Center the ribbon over the raw edges of the quilt piece, and pin in place. Topstitch the ribbon along both long edges using a ⅛" seam allowance. (The bobbin thread will show on the right side of the bracelet, so you may wish to use a bobbin with a complementary color thread.) Press on both sides.

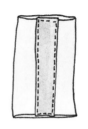

5. Join the short ends of the bracelet, and pin together so that they touch but do not overlap. Sew the short ends together by hand.

6. Apply a small amount of fabric glue to both sides of the seam that joins the bracelet, and adhere a piece of decorative ribbon to wrap around and cover that seam on both sides. Allow the glue to dry before wearing.

No-Sew Patchwork Wreath

A wreath on your front door is a welcome sign that greets passersby, and it is also a nice way to display a treasured quilt. My love for patchwork wreaths dates back to a beloved family ornament that hung on our holiday tree throughout my childhood. Its simple design resurfaced in my work over the years in the form of many sewn patchwork wreaths sold in my shop. To make this no-sew variation, simply look around the house for the necessary materials, and rescue a section of your favorite cutter quilt to create a lovely decoration for your home.

. . . .

FINISHED MEASUREMENTS

16" in diameter

WHAT YOU NEED

- One cutter quilt
- Foam swimming noodle cut to 48" length
- Straight pins
- Thimble (optional, but highly recommended if you have one)
- One set of takeout chopsticks
- Duct tape
- Embroidery floss or ribbon to hang

HOW TO MAKE

1. Lay out your cutter quilt face up to determine what section you would like to salvage for your wreath. Don't worry about any threadbare bits since they will add charm to the finished piece.

2. Starting at an edge, roll the foam noodle in the quilt until the fabric overlaps itself by about 3" to establish your width measurement. Cut a piece from the quilt that is the determined width measurement by the length of 51", or 3" longer than the noodle.

3. Lay the noodle straight along the wrong side of the quilt piece with 3" of the quilt extending beyond one end of the noodle.

4. Use straight pins to secure one long edge of the quilt along the length of the noodle. Insert the pins straight through the quilt and into the noodle every 2" or so.

5. Roll the noodle in the quilt until the fabric overlaps itself snugly. Secure the quilt to itself and the noodle with straight pins along the length of the noodle just as before. (If you prefer not having the raw edge exposed, fold the raw edge under as you pin.)

6. When you have almost completed wrapping the entire noodle with the cutter quilt piece, create the wreath form by inserting the chopsticks (packaging and all) halfway into the hole at one end of the noodle. Place the other end of the noodle over the chopsticks that are sticking out of the other end to join the noodle. Use duct tape to secure the noodle closed.

7. Continue wrapping the quilt back around the noodle as before, and secure it in place with pins. Add additional pins to secure any gaps as needed.

8. Wrap a strand of embroidery floss or ribbon around the wreath to hang it up for display.

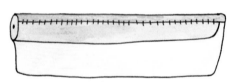
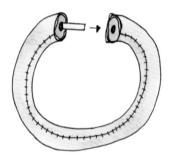

Hanayo Bag

One summer while taking professional development courses in Germany, I had the pleasure of sharing a student apartment with a lovely teacher from Japan named Hanayo. It was a wonderful opportunity to further our studies as foreign-language teachers, while also learning more about our unique cultures from each other. I always admired her terrific sense of style and ultimately created this simple shoulder bag thinking it might be something she would carry. I find that incorporating fabric from a cutter quilt juxtaposes nicely with the petite shape. It is a coming together of styles, much as Hanayo and I were all those many years ago.

. . . .

FINISHED MEASUREMENTS

10" × 7½" (although you can easily enlarge the pattern to create a larger bag)

WHAT YOU NEED

- Hanayo Bag pattern piece (found in the Resources section of this book)
- Cutter quilt pieces: (2 pieces) about 10" × 12"
- Linen or cotton fabric for the lining: (2 pieces) about 10" × 12"
- Walking foot for your sewing machine (optional, but very helpful)
- Cotton webbing for the strap: (1 piece) 25" × 1"
- Embroidery floss
- Elastic cord for the closure (such as a ponytail elastic)
- One vintage button

HOW TO MAKE

Note: Backstitch beginning and end of each line of stitches.

1. Use the pattern piece to cut two pieces from the cutter quilt and two pieces from the lining fabric. Consider placement of any favorite motif, print, or patchwork block on your bag when laying out the pattern piece for cutting. Carefully cut out the darts in the lower corners according to the pattern piece as well.

2. Working with one of the cutter quilt pieces, pin the cut edges of each of the two darts right sides together. Using a ¼" seam allowance, sew together working from the inside toward the edge. This method creates a slightly rounded gusset rather than a flat bag.

3. Press the seam open on the wrong side, and then press again on the right side. Repeat this step with the other cutter quilt piece, as well as with both lining pieces.

4. Now is a great time to add a bit of hand embroidery to the quilted fabrics, if you like. Consider using the prints as a guide when selecting colors and placement of your embroidery. It is amazing what a bit of running stitch can add to a piece like this one. Another idea would be simply to add a bit of cross-stitch at the seams. Use your imagination, and enjoy the idea of adding your stitches to this well-loved piece of vintage handwork.

5. Place the exterior quilted pieces right sides together, and pin along the entire curved edge. Using a ¼" seam allowance, sew them together along that curved edge. Press the seams open on the wrong side, and then turn right side out and press again on the right side.

6. Repeat for the lining pieces, but leave a 3" opening along the bottom for turning.

7. Turn the quilted piece inside out, and place the strap inside. Place the ends of the strap at the side seams with the ends extended past the top edge, and pin in place. Using a ¼" seam allowance to sew the straps in place at the seams.

8. Pin a loop of elastic cord to the center of what will be the back of the bag, leaving the majority of the elastic looping down toward the bottom of the bag. Stitch in place to the right side of the bag using a ¼" seam allowance.

9. With the bag still inside out and the lining right side out, place the lining inside of the bag so that they are right sides together and the strap and elastic closure are nestled in between both. Pin together around the entire top edge of the bag and lining, taking time to carefully line up the seams. Using a ½" seam allowance, sew the bag and the lining together. Press along the entire top seam to set the stitches.

10. Carefully reach inside the bag through the opening in the lining to turn the bag right side out. Gently pull the strap out as well as the elastic closure. Reach inside between the lining and exterior fabric to press into the curved seams with your hand.

11. Pin the opening in the lining closed, and secure it by machine stitching with a ⅛" seam allowance or sewing a blind stitch by hand.

12. Place the lining inside the bag, and press the entire top edge of the bag with an iron. Topstitch using a ¼" seam allowance to secure the lining to the bag exterior along that top edge. Carefully press the entire bag with an iron to set all the stitches.

13. Loop the elastic cord over the front edge of the bag, and mark where appropriate placement of the button should be. Stitch your button in place by hand.

Mini-Project: Quilty Carabiner Case

I love the idea of combining vintage materials with modern elements, especially when making small accessories. One example is this sweet little mobile phone case made from cutter quilt scraps. The carabiner allows you to clip the case onto your belt or bag so it is at the ready to connect you with the world when needed, but it will not cramp your vintage-modern-loving style.

To Make: Create a rectangular pattern piece 1" larger than your mobile phone on all sides, and use it to cut two pieces of cutter quilt and two lining pieces. Follow the basic construction method as for the Hanayo Bag (without the strap) to create a small pouch, and attach a loop of ribbon instead of the elastic cord. When finished, hook the carabiner through the ribbon loop, slip your phone inside, clip in place, and you are good to go!

Vintage Pillowcases & Sheeting

The soft florals of vintage sheeting remind me of childhood visits to my grandparents' home on a quiet lake in northeastern Pennsylvania. I fondly remember digging for worms under the slate footpath, fishing on the dock, swimming in the channel, watching Grampa make dollhouse furniture in his tiny cellar wood shop, playing bingo at the marina, ice-skating in winter on the bumpy surface of the frozen water, and rocking with Grammy on their porch glider. At the end of the day, everyone would collapse into beds made up with soft old-fashioned sheets, drifting off to sleep, exhausted and happy.

Vintage sheeting is a wonderful alternative to traditional fabrics to use in your sewing. There are so many colorful and pretty patterns out there, and this affordable option is readily available at thrift stores. Incorporating vintage sheeting with its soft colors and old-fashioned prints brings a breath of fresh air to your handmade projects and calls to mind the simple pleasures like gathering fresh wash from the line, pillow fights, and the smell of lilacs wafting through the air in springtime—the good old days.

Stashbuster Steering Wheel Cover

Stylize your ride with this whimsical steering wheel cover featuring a patchwork of colorful vintage prints. Made using bits and pieces of your favorite old-fashioned sheeting, this is a fun way to bring some charm and personality to your car. And it will surely take the ho-hum out of running errands.

FINISHED MEASUREMENTS

Approximately 49" in circumference with stretchy sides to fit a standard car steering wheel

WHAT YOU NEED

- Vintage sheeting in a variety of complementary prints: (15 pieces) 3" × 4"
- Linen or cotton fabric in a complementary color: (2 pieces) 2" × 50"
- Nonskid fabric: (1 piece) 3" × 50" (the same material used on the soles of footy pajamas)
- 1"-wide ribbon: (1 piece) 3" in length
- ¼" elastic: (2 pieces) 40" in length
- Walking foot for your sewing machine (optional, but very helpful)

HOW TO MAKE

Note: Backstitch beginning and end of each line of stitches.

1. Place two of the 3" × 4" pieces right sides together, and pin along one of the 3" sides. Sew these pieces together along the pinned 3" side using a ¼" seam allowance. Press the seams to one side on the wrong side, and then press again on the right side.
2. Sew together all of the 3" × 4" pieces in this manner, connecting them along their 3" sides to create one long strip of patchwork. When finished, press on both sides then cut the strip to a length of 50".
3. Pin the patchwork to the nonskid fabric piece, with wrong sides together. Sew together on all sides using a ¼" seam allowance.

4. Place one of the 2" × 50" complementary fabric strips on top of the patchwork, with right sides facing, and pin along one long edge. Sew the long edge using a ½" seam allowance. Carefully press over the seam on the right side of the sheeting fabrics only. Be extra careful not to iron the nonskid fabric directly because it could melt onto the surface of your iron. Repeat with the second 2" × 50" fabric piece along the other long side edge of the patchwork.

5. Pin the two short ends with patchwork sides together to form a continuous loop. Sew along the edge using a ½" seam allowance. Finger press the nonskid fabric seam open on the wrong side.

6. Center the piece of ribbon directly on top of this seam, and pin in place. Topstitch the ribbon in place on all sides using a ⅛" seam allowance.

7. Working on a flat surface with the nonskid side facing up, fold one long fabric edge over ½" toward the wrong side as you would the hem of a skirt. Press, and then fold it over again, aligning the pressed edge with the existing side seam, and pin in place around the entire circumference of the piece. (This will become the casing for the elastic.) Topstitch the casing on the back side of the piece using a ⅛" seam allowance, leaving a 2" opening for the elastic. Repeat this process to create the casing for the other circular edge of the piece.

8. Feed the elastic through the casing, being careful not to twist, and securely stitch it to itself. Repeat for the other side.

9. Sew both casings closed in line with the topstitching, using a ⅛" seam allowance.

10. At this point, it will appear bunched and twisty, but in reality, it is all done and ready to be stretched over your steering wheel!

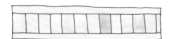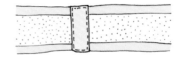

Fruit-Striped Circle Scarf

I love the look of combining different bands of vintage sheeting to create cheery-colored stripes. Years ago, I purchased a pillow featuring a similar pastel rainbow of colors made by Sparkle Power designer and friend, Candace Todd. Her piecework was understated, and the contrast of soft colors was so lovely. I wanted to re-create those stripes in some sort of accessory to wear, and ultimately came up with this infinity scarf. I like to line these scarves with lightweight knit cotton to be worn throughout the seasons. Think of it as that little extra bit of sunshine you can enjoy every day of the year.

FINISHED MEASUREMENTS

9" × 50" in circumference

WHAT YOU NEED

- Vintage pillowcases a rainbow of fruity colors
- Soft fabric for scarf lining, such as a lightweight cotton knit, flannel, or linen: (1 piece) 10" × 51"

HOW TO MAKE

Note: Backstitch beginning and end of each line of stitches.

1. Cut your pillowcase fabrics into 12" long strips of varying widths (1½"–3").
2. Working on a flat surface, arrange the strips in a pleasing colorful pattern. Sew the strips together using a ¼" seam allowance to create a 51" long piece of colorful striped patchwork. Press the seams to one side on the wrong side, and then press again on the right side.
3. Since the patchwork will likely have shifted somewhat during the piecing process, straighten out the edges of the patchwork by trimming as needed so your patchwork is 10" wide.
4. Sew the two short ends of the striped patchwork right sides together using a ½" seam allowance. Press the seam to one side on the wrong side, and then press again on the right side.

5. Sew the two short ends of the lining fabric right sides together using a ½" seam allowance. Press the seam to one side on the wrong side, and then press again on the right side.

6. Turn the patchwork so that the wrong side is facing out, and then place the lining fabric inside of the patchwork so that the right sides are together. Align the top circular edges, and pin together around the circumference. Sew the top edges together using a ½" seam allowance. Press on both sides.

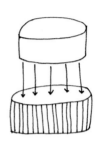

7. Turn the piece right side out, and place the lining and patchwork so wrong sides are together. Press along the seam around the top edge. Topstitch around the entire top circumference using a ¼" seam allowance. Press the topstitching on both sides.

8. Fold the bottom circular edge of the patchwork ½" toward the wrong side, and press with an iron. Repeat for the bottom circular edge of the lining. Align those bottom edges, and pin together. Topstitch around the entire bottom circumference using a ¼" seam allowance. Press on both sides.

Mini-Project: Under-the-Rainbow Garland

A fun way to welcome people into your home is to drape small-scale garlands leading from your entranceway into your living space or even incorporate them into your garden. Switching out the colors according to holidays and seasons is simple to do, and this is a fun project you can create together with your family. This rainbow garland was made using the leftover strips of vintage sheeting, but you can use any leftover fabrics you have on hand to create a sweet bit of welcoming decor for your home.

To Make: Cut narrow strips of fabric into 8"–12" lengths. This piece was made using leftover fabric strips from making the Fruit-Striped Circle Scarf (page 69) and Now-and-Then iPad Sleeve (page 76). Tie the strips together to achieve your desired length. Then tape to the ceiling with a slight drape, or tie to branches in the garden to create a colorful cascade throughout your home.

Sun-in-the-Morning Baby Quilt

One of our favorite songs to sing at the top of our lungs in the car (or anywhere, for that matter) is the Irving Berlin classic "I Got the Sun in the Morning" from Annie, Get Your Gun. That song came to mind one afternoon as I looked at the growing pile of golds and yellows while stacking freshly laundered vintage bed linens at my studio. It was a pile of sunshine! I designed this quilted patchwork blanket—inspired by the song, the lovely golden tones, and my children—for you to make and share with your own little sunshines.

. . . .

FINISHED MEASUREMENTS

Approximately 37" × 50"

WHAT YOU NEED

- 6 vintage pillowcases in yellow prints with backgrounds graduating from deep gold to white, cut into 48 squares, each measuring 8" × 8" as follows:

  darkest tone (1)—4 pieces
  next darkest tone (2)—10 pieces
  middle dark tone (3)—12 pieces
  middle light tone (4)—10 pieces
  second lightest color (5)—8 pieces
  lightest color (6)—4 pieces

- Soft fabric for the blanket backing, such as cotton fleece, flannel, and minky fabric cut slightly larger than the pieced quilt top: (1 piece) 40" × 53" (Be sure to prewash the backing fabric to allow for shrinkage prior to cutting to size.)
- 100% cotton hand- or machine-quilting thread in a complementary color

HOW TO MAKE

Note: Backstitch beginning and end of each line of stitches.

1. Following the directions in the Stitch Guide (page 123), create 48 7" half-square triangles using the following color combinations:

- 4 squares each of colors 1+2 to make 8 pieces; we will refer to this as A
- 6 squares each of colors 2+3 to make 12 pieces; we will refer to this as B
- 6 squares each of colors 3+4 to make 12 pieces; we will refer to this as C
- 4 squares each of colors 4+5 to make 8 pieces; we will refer to this as D
- 4 squares each of colors 5+6 to make 8 pieces; we will refer to this as E

2. Arrange your half-square triangles on a flat surface according to the illustration. Sew the squares together using a ¼" seam allowance. As you go, press the seams to alternating sides and open in order to reduce bulk, and then press again on the right side.

3. Once your quilt top has been completely pieced, press it well on both sides.

4. Smooth out your backing fabric on a flat surface with right side facing up, and then place the quilt top on top of the backing with the right side facing down. It is okay if the backing fabric piece is slightly larger than the pieced quilt top; simply cut the backing fabric to size, using the quilt top as a guide. Pin the front and back together around the entire perimeter of the blanket with right sides together. Sew around all four sides using a ½" seam allowance, leaving an 8" opening for turning. Press on both sides to set the stitches.

5. Reach through the opening to turn the piece right sides out. Gently press into the corners with your finger. Pin the opening closed and topstitch around the entire perimeter of the piece using a ¼" seam allowance, securing that opening in the process.

6. Use cotton quilting thread to hand or machine quilt the blanket with a sunrise pattern, such as the one shown in the illustration. Or simply use your imagination to create a quilt pattern that makes you smile. It will be absolutely lovely, I am sure!

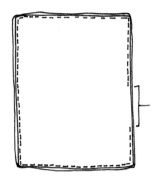

Now-and-Then iPad Sleeve

For many of us, reminiscences of childhood are uncomplicated by gadgetry. Some of my most special memories are of summer vacations spent at Pine Aire Cottages in the Adirondack Mountains of upstate New York. Learning to fish, toes sinking into the soft bottom of the lake while we swam, boat rides, cards games, clambakes, and nightly campfires—there was not a telephone or television to speak of, and no one was complaining. It was truly time away from it all. This was long before the age of Wi-Fi and being connected with the world 24/7. Sometimes I wonder what our then-selves would think about recent advances in technology. True, we all can appreciate what modern technology has to offer, and we all most certainly enjoy a bit of screen time now and then—it has its place. But we also use our power to unplug and put these devices away, as well. For the times when you choose to put it in its place, slip your tablet into its very own log cabin—away from it all.

FINISHED MEASUREMENTS

Approximately 8" × 10"

WHAT YOU NEED

- Vintage textile fussy cut motif, such as a bit of hand-embroidery: (2 pieces) 3" × 3"
- Vintage sheeting cut into 1½"-wide strips in a variety of colors and prints
- Cotton quilt batting: (2 pieces) 11" × 11"
- Vintage sheeting for the lining: (2 pieces) 9" × 11"
- Walking foot for your sewing machine (optional, but very helpful)

HOW TO MAKE

Note: Backstitch beginning and end of each line of stitches.

In this project, we will be using a popular method of quilting I first learned about in Suzuko Koseki's book *Patchwork Style* and later saw featured by Amanda Soule on her blog *SouleMama*. You use this method, often called "quilt as you go," to stitch your fabrics directly to a piece of batting and, as the name suggests, quilt as you go, and then trim the piece to size for assembly. There is no need to use backing fabric because you will create a lining piece later. Also, it is especially fun to look at the reverse of the batting to appreciate all your lovely lines of quilting!

1. Place one piece of quilt batting on your work surface. Position one of the fussy cut squares in the center of the batting tilted as a diamond with its right side facing up, and pin in place. Stitch the square down on all four sides using a ¼" seam allowance, securing it to the batting. Press on the right side.

2. Cut a 3" length of one of the fabric strips. Place this strip on top of the center square with right sides facing each other, aligning their 3" sides. Sew the fabrics together using a ¼" seam allowance, and then finger press the seam open. Quilt the strip down to the batting using ¼" straight-line quilting. Press on the right side.

3. Continue adding strips in this manner, building layers of increasing length around the log cabin sides in a diamond formation as you go. Each time, sew the new strip to the block with right sides facing, finger press the seam open, and then sew it down using ¼" straight-line quilting on the right side.

4. When the log cabin diamond block is filled, trim the excess fabric to a piece that measures 9" wide × 11" high, with the embroidery centered in the piece. Press on both sides. Repeat with the other fabrics to create a second log cabin block for the back.

5. Place the two quilt blocks right sides together, and pin together both sides and the bottom edge. Sew those three sides together using a ⅜" seam allowance. Clip the bottom corners on an angle to reduce bulk. Press on both sides, but leave the block wrong side out and set aside.

6. Place the two lining pieces right sides together, and pin both sides and the bottom edge. Sew those three sides together using a ⅜" seam allowance, leaving a 4" opening along the bottom edge for turning. Press on both sides, and clip the bottom corners on an angle to reduce bulk. Turn right side out, and press again.

7. Place the lining inside the exterior quilted sleeve so that the top edges are aligned and their right sides are together. Pin around the top edge, and then sew it together using a ⅜" seam allowance. Press on both sides, and then reach through the opening to turn the piece right side out.

8. Pin the opening in the lining, and sew it closed using a ⅛" seam allowance.

9. Using a ¼" seam allowance, topstitch around the entire top edge, and then press on both sides. Slip your iPad inside, and enjoy a bit of time unplugged.

Mini-Project: Stylus Strap

The idea for this little strap came from one too many lost stylus pens, along with a desire to keep my iPad safely tucked inside its case when not in use. This strap is simple to make and pulls the whole thing together beautifully. This also works wonderfully as a pen sleeve wrapped around a sketchbook or journal.

To Make: Form a loop with a 17" length of 1" elastic, and pin it lengthwise to a 2¼" × 6¾" piece of 3 mm thick wool felt. Secure the elastic to the felt by sewing up and down both sides. Take a 4½" × 6½" piece of leftover patchwork from another project, and fold it in half lengthwise with right sides together so it measures 2¼" × 6½". Sew the long side and one short end together using a ¼" seam allowance. Clip the corners, and turn it right side out and press again. Fold the open edges under ¼" toward the inside of the piece, and pin it to the right side of the felt with the open edge centered at the bottom. Topstitch the fabric piece to the felt along both long sides and the bottom using a ⅛" seam allowance. Stretch the strap over your iPad sleeve, and tuck the stylus in its sleeve when not in use.

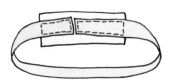

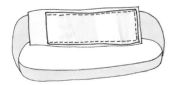

Spring Garden Canisters

For many of us, springtime makes us want to clean out and organize our homes. These canisters are a simple storage solution you can easily create using materials from around the house. Using the cheery prints of vintage sheeting is perfect for spring, and if you like, you can make the reverse side using other fabrics and simply swap them out for a different look whenever you wish.

FINISHED MEASUREMENTS

Whatever size you like

WHAT YOU NEED

- Vintage pillowcases and sheeting fabrics in a variety of colorful prints
- Paper-backed fusible web (such as Wonder Under or HeatnBond)
- Empty canisters (such as those from oatmeal, tea, coffee, cornmeal, peanut butter)
- ¾" wide sticky-back hook-and-loop tape (such as Velcro)

HOW TO MAKE

1. Measure the height of each canister, making ¼" allowances for the top and bottom edges. Then measure the circumference of the canister, adding an additional 1" (this part will overlap with the hook-and-loop tape).
2. Follow the manufacturer's instruction on the fusible web to adhere the wrong sides of two fabrics to each other. (Consider when you might like to swap out the fabrics on these canisters in the future—use something festive for the holidays, perhaps?)
3. Use your canister measurements to cut a rectangular piece from the fused fabrics.
4. Adhere a piece of hook-and-loop tape to one short end of the fabric on the right side. Then adhere the corresponding piece of hook-and-loop tape to the other short end of the fabric on the wrong side.
5. Wrap the fabric band around the canister and overlap the ends, using the hook-and-loop tape to secure it to itself and the canister.

6. To feature the reverse fabric, simply unfasten the closure, flip over the fabric, and secure the hook-and-loop tape to itself with the opposite fabric facing out. If you prefer a more permanent effect, you can glue the fabric ends together around the canister using a strong fabric glue. Then simply cover the seam with decorative ribbon.

Aprons

Over the past several years, vintage-inspired aprons have seen a resurgence in popularity and have become trendy retro-style accessories to make and wear. True vintage aprons are also highly sought-after collectibles many adore for their sentimental qualities. Handmade aprons possess inspiring, one-of-a-kind details and craftsmanship, such as hand-stitched smocking, embroidered monograms, frilly lace hemlines, repurposed silkscreened kitchen towels, flowery feed-sack prints, and so much more. I often come across worn or torn aprons while treasure hunting. Despite their wear and tear, they are still quite charming and lovely. With all their wonderful fabrics and one-of-a-kind handwork, aprons are fantastic materials to repurpose and incorporate into sewing modern pieces that highlight all their charming bits.

Keepsake Diary

There is something to be said for putting pen to paper. Whether for class notes, shopping lists, planning blog posts, or journaling your innermost thoughts—pen on paper means something. At the top of my list of favorite journals is the classic composition notebook with the hardcover that protects its pages. More than twenty years ago, I deconstructed and repurposed a vintage apron to create a stitched cover similar to this one for my trusty composition notebook, transforming it into something truly special. That same cover has protected dozens of notebooks over the years, and I still use it every day. My hope is that this diary cover will be a treasured keepsake for you, as well.

FINISHED MEASUREMENTS

Approximately 9¾" × 15¼"

WHAT YOU NEED

- Two complementary vintage aprons (one with a pocket for the front, one without for the back)
- ½" rickrack: (1 piece) 12" in length
- One standard composition notebook

HOW TO MAKE

Note: Backstitch beginning and end of each line of stitches.

1. Use a seam ripper or small scissors to remove the straps from both aprons carefully. If either apron has a gathered skirt, remove the skirt section from the top of the apron to create a smooth piece of fabric free of pleats and gathers. Press the straps and skirt fabric pieces. Set the straps aside for later use.
2. Working with the front apron fabric right side up, cut a piece that is 14½" wide × 11" high; be sure the pocket is centered vertically and within 2" to 3" of the left edge.
3. Pin the rickrack to the right side of the fabric along the left 11" edge, aligning it ⅛" in from the edge. Topstitch it in place using a ¼" seam allowance.
4. Cut a piece from the back apron fabric that is also 14½" × 11".

5. Place both fabrics right sides together, and pin along the short edge with the rickrack. Sew together along this one edge using a ⅜" seam allowance. Press the seam open on the wrong side, and then press again on the right side.

6. Working on a flat surface with the wrong side facing up, fold one of the short edges over ½" toward the wrong side as you would the hem of a skirt. Press, and then fold it over itself another ½" and press again. Topstitch this folded short edge using a ¼" seam allowance. Press on both the wrong and right sides. Repeat this step for the other short edge.

7. Take your composition notebook and place it on the wrong side of the apron fabric, aligning the spine along the seam joining the front and back fabrics. Fold the fabric for the front over the front cover of the notebook. Pull the fabric taut, and turn the extra fabric to the inside front cover of the notebook so that the pocket is aligned on the front cover. Finger crease the folded edge along the edge of the notebook cover.

8. Using the crease as a guide, pin one of the apron straps to the front cover with the raw edge facing toward the crease and the length of the strap extending toward the spine seam, centering the strap vertically. Sew the strap to the front cover using a ¼" seam allowance. Press, and then fold the strap back over itself along that ¼" seam so that the strap is now extending toward the edge of the front cover; pin in place. Topstitch the strap in place, ⅛" in from the seam. Repeat for the back cover strap, making sure the front and back cover straps align.

9. When sewing the front and back flaps, work with the right side of the fabric facing up. Align the binding of your composition notebook along the seam that joins the front and back fabrics. Fold the front panel over the book to inside the front cover, and fold the back panel over the other cover. Close the notebook to ensure the fabric is taut and the pocket is centered vertically, and then pin the top and bottom edges together. Remove the notebook so you can sew the top pinned edge using a ½" seam allowance. Repeat for the bottom edge. Press on both sides, including the straps.

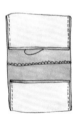

10. Fit the notebook cover over your composition notebook, and tie the straps to keep everything in place.

Criss-Cross Coasters

The very first patchwork I remember making as a young girl was a nine-patch pillow that earned me a merit badge in sewing. This simple design is a nod to times past, and also a creative way to repurpose treasured textiles. Over the years, a plus-sign graphic is something I have featured when making quilts because, to me, this symbol celebrates the positive. It also translates well when miniaturized in a stack of quilted coasters. These are made using fabrics from vintage apron straps, but any combination of scraps from your favorite textiles would look equally lovely.

FINISHED MEASUREMENTS

4" × 4"

WHAT YOU NEED (FOR ONE COASTER)

- Straps from two complementary vintage aprons: (2 pieces each of fabrics A and B) 2" × 4½"
- Sturdy fabric for the reverse, such as linen or tablecloth fabrics: (1 piece) 4½" × 4½"
- Cotton quilt batting: (1 piece) 4½" × 4½"

HOW TO MAKE

Note: Backstitch beginning and end of each line of stitches.

1. With right sides together, sew one piece of fabric A to one piece of fabric B along one long side using a ¼" seam allowance. Then sew the other piece of fabric A to the other long side of that same B piece. Press the seams to one side on the wrong side, and press again on the right side.

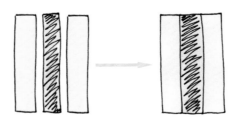

2. Cut the patchwork in half, dividing it into two ABA pieces. Place one patchwork strip on top of the second B piece with right sides together, and pin along one long edge. Sew them together using a ¼" seam allowance. Repeat with the other patchwork strip on the other long B side. Press the seams to one side on the wrong side, and press again on the right side. (Voilà, a plus sign!) Trim the square to be 4½" × 4½".

3. Place the square of quilt batting on your work surface, place the patchwork block on top of it with the right side facing up, and then place the backing fabric on the very top of the pile with the right side facing down. Pin on all four sides. Use a ¼" seam allowance to sew around the perimeter of the square, leaving a 2" opening for turning. Press on the wrong side of the backing fabric to set the stitches.

4. Clip the corners, and then turn right side out through the opening and carefully press into the corners with a chopstick or bone folder. Turn the edges at the opening to the inside, aligning the opening with the edge of the coaster; press and pin shut. Topstitch around all four sides of the coaster using a ⅛" seam allowance, securing the opening closed in the process. Press on both sides.

5. Use straight-line stitches to quilt ⅛" on either side of the criss-cross seams, if you like, or simply keep as is. Make a stack of coasters in this manner using fabric scraps.

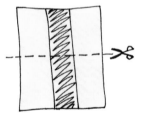 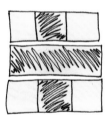

Mini-Project: Accentuate-the-Positive Adjustable Belt

No matter what your shape or size, almost every garment is instantly more flattering when belted. Making a belt is one of those things you may have never done, and the process will surprise you with its simplicity, as well as the good-looking results. The patchwork uses the same plus-sign graphic of the Criss-Cross Coasters (page 87) on an even smaller scale, allowing you to accentuate your curves.

To Make: Create miniature plus-sign patchwork blocks using 1" × 3" vintage fabric strips. Use the same piecing method as in the Criss-Cross Coaster project. Measure your waistline, adding 8" to the number to get the total length needed for your belt. Sew your patchwork plus-sign pieces together using a ¼" seam allowance, interspersing them with strips of linen or complementary fabric. Cut a piece of coordinating fabric for the reverse of the belt, and pin it to the patchwork at both short ends and one long side with right sides together. Using a ¼" seam allowance, sew those three sides together. Press on both sides, and then turn right side out and press again. Turn the long raw edges under ¼" toward the inside, and pin closed. Topstitch around all four sides using a ⅛" seam allowance, and in the process, you will secure that long edge closed. Press on both sides. Feed 1" of one end through two D-rings, and loop it over to pin it to itself with wrong sides together. Sew the belt end in place so the D-rings are secure for wear.

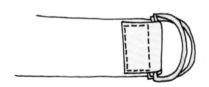

Paneled Twirly Skirt

We all love easy-to-wear clothes—pieces you need not worry about pressing, that you can just slip on and pair with a T-shirt and look great every time. This paneled skirt was inspired by the work of Kinchi designer Mirjam Bos, who years ago made a few wonderful A-line skirts for my daughters featuring vintage fabrics from the Netherlands. I like to incorporate vintage aprons in these simple paneled skirts to give them a charming '50s feel, reminiscent of Donna Reed. You can make these in any size and for any age by simply lengthening the skirt and adding additional fabric panels to fit as needed. I imagine that, like us, you and your loved ones will have several of these skirts in your wardrobes very soon.

. . . .

FINISHED MEASUREMENTS

Project shown 15½" long with an elasticized waistline sized to fit a child aged 6–10 years old (But you can easily size this to fit just about anyone of any age.)

WHAT YOU NEED

- 2 vintage aprons with a goodly amount of fabric and of approximately the same length
- ¾" elastic: (1 piece) the length of the wearer's waist minus 2"

Note: If making this for an adult, you may need three aprons depending on the amount of fabric in each apron and size of wearer. Be sure to take measurements of the wearer and fabrics, and have extra aprons on hand, as needed.

HOW TO MAKE

Note: Backstitch beginning and end of each line of stitches.

1. Use a seam ripper or small scissors to carefully remove the straps and waistbands from two aprons, and set them aside for use in other projects. (You can use the apron straps to create a coordinating Strappy Hair Band, as seen on page 94.)
2. If either apron has a pocket, remove it with a seam ripper at this point, and set it aside to be sewn onto the skirt once the panels have been pieced. Smooth out

the skirt sections from both aprons, and then press all the apron fabrics on both sides.

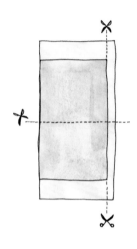

3. Place the two apron fabrics one on top of the other with the hemlines aligned. Cut off any excess at the top if one piece is slightly longer than the other one. Then cut both pieces in half from top to bottom. (Do not worry if the fabric pieces from your aprons have different widths—a bit of asymmetry adds charm.)

4. With the hemlines of the apron fabrics aligned, place one panel of apron A on top of one panel of apron B with right sides together. Pin along one side, from waist to hem. Sew together using a ⅜" seam allowance. Overlock, serge, or use a zigzag stitch to prevent fraying. Press the seam to one side on the wrong side, and then press again on the right side.

5. Repeat this step exactly as before using the other two apron panels. Then join those two pieces in the same manner as with the individual panels. You should have one long piece containing four alternating panels of your two aprons. Measure the waist of the intended wearer—the long paneled piece should measure about twice that of the intended wearer's waist. (If needed, add an additional panel from another apron.)

6. If you previously removed a pocket from one of the aprons, now is the time to sew it in place on the skirt. Position the pocket right side up, over one of the seams and centered from top to bottom. Pin on both sides as well as along the bottom, and then topstitch in place using a ⅛" seam allowance. Press on both sides.

7. Pin the sides of the skirt right sides together from waist to hem, and sew together using a ⅜" seam allowance. Overlock, serge, or zigzag stitch to prevent fraying. Press the seam to one side on the wrong side, and then press again on the right side.

8. Fold the top edge of the waistband over ¼" toward the wrong side and press. Then fold it over again, this time folding it over 1¼". Press this top fold, which will become the top of the waistband casing. I recommend that you topstitch along this fold using a ⅛" seam allowance to help the elastic from twisting about when the skirt is worn. Pin the waistband to the skirt to create the casing for the elastic. Using a ⅛" seam allowance, topstitch along the bottom edge of the waistband all the way around the skirt, leaving a few inches open to insert the elastic. Press on both sides.

9. Slip the elastic through the waistband casing, being careful not to twist. Overlap the ends of the elastic by 1", and sew them together using a zigzag stitch. Tug the waistband to allow the elastic to slip into place.

10. Topstitch the casing opening closed using a ⅛" seam allowance, as before. Then topstitch the hemline using a ¼" seam allowance to help keep the seams down, as well as give the hem a finished look. Press on both sides, and it is ready to wear!

Strappy Hair Bands

Long tresses look retro chic when pulled back with fabric ties from vintage aprons. These great hair bands have a hidden bit of elastic at the nape of your neck to ensure a perfect fit every time without having to tie the top knot just so again and again. Easy to make and without a stitch of sewing involved, a bunch of these strappy hair bands can be whipped up quickly to keep you accessorized and your hair styled every day of the week.

FINISHED MEASUREMENTS

Sized to fit the wearer

WHAT YOU NEED

- Two straps from a vintage apron
- One ponytail hair elastic

HOW TO MAKE

1. Press the apron straps on both sides. Each apron strap should have one good/finished end and one raw end from where it was removed from the apron skirt. Use the good ends to tie a decorative knot (which will ultimately sit atop your head).
2. Measure the size of your head from the crown, down behind your ears, and all the way to the nape of your neck (where the hair band will sit).
3. Place the fabric on your work surface, and cut it to size with the knot positioned accordingly.

4. Make a knot in the hair elastic so that it looks like a knotted figure eight.
5. Slip one end of the fabric through one loop of the elastic, and tie a knot. Repeat with the other end through the other loop.
6. Try on the hair band, and make adjustments in fit as needed.

Mini-Project: Book Worm Paperweight

There are times you would really benefit from an extra set of hands to hold a book open, like when you are cooking, knitting, or perhaps sewing. Enter this simple book weight that you can put together in a flash—and without a stitch of sewing, either.

To Make: Cut a 12" length from a portion of a vintage apron that has two layers of fabric that form a tube (such as the waistband casing or hemline). One end should be securely closed, but the other raw end should be open, giving access to the fabric tube. Fill it ¾ full with dried beans, and then seal the remaining fabric at the opening together with fusible web (such as Wonder Under, HeatnBond, Steam-A-Seam, and Stitch Witchery) or fabric glue (such as Fabri-Tac). With the beans pushed into the piece as much as possible, fold the excess fabric down over the piece, and then adhere a piece of decorative ribbon over the raw edge and around the entire piece using fabric glue. When dry, place the paperweight across the pages of your open book while you get back to business.

This Song Is about You Pillow

Do you have a treasured apron that someone in your family used to wear? Is there a special song that calls that person to mind? Song lyrics can trigger specific memories, or simply cause us to ponder their meaning in the right here right now of our lives. This project is a textile tattoo of sorts; you combine hand-stitched appliqué of meaningful-to-you lyrics with pretty, vintage apron fabrics to create this lovely and very personal bit of home decor. Ours is a "Dear Prudence" pillow, but yours can reference whatever song you like. Make one in honor of someone special to your family, or simply because the lyrics resonate with you and yours.

. . . .

FINISHED MEASUREMENTS

20" × 20"

WHAT YOU NEED

- Vintage fabrics (such as those from treasured family aprons): (1 front piece) 21" × 21" and (2 back pieces) 21" × 16"
- Linen fabric for the appliqué: (1 piece) about 10" × 10"
- Water-soluble fabric marking pen
- Embroidery floss in contrasting colors
- Embroidery hoop (optional, but very helpful)
- Paper-backed fusible web (such as Wonder Under or HeatnBond)
- ½" double fold bias tape in a coordinating color: 4 yards
- 20" × 20" pillow form

HOW TO MAKE

Note: Backstitch beginning and end of each line of stitches.

1. Study your larger fabric piece to consider how your chosen lyrics can connect with the color palette of your fabrics and embroidery floss. Use a water-soluble fabric marking pen to write your lyrics directly onto the linen piece, along with any additional designs you wish to incorporate. (If you would like to incorporate a particular font for this piece, type the text into a computer first and print a copy to use for tracing. You don't need a fancy light box—simply tape the

paper copy to a window with the fabric positioned atop it, and use the daylight to help trace your text onto the linen.)

2. Place this fabric in the embroidery hoop, and stitch the lyrics onto the fabric with embroidery floss. (Refer to the Stitch Guide on pages 121–22 for examples of basic embroidery stitches.) When finished, spritz the pen markings with water to make the ink disappear from the fabric. Allow to dry, and press carefully on both sides.

3. Apply the paper-backed fusible web according to the manufacturer's instructions to the back side of the embroidered linen fabric to be appliquéd. Cut it to the desired shape. When cool, remove the paper backing and adhere the appliqué to the main pillow fabric piece, following the manufacturer's instructions. Topstitch around the raw edge of the appliqué using a ⅛" seam allowance. Press on both sides and set aside.

4. Pin a 21" length of bias tape over the raw edge of one long side on one smaller (back) fabric piece. Using a ⅜" seam allowance, sew the bias tape to the fabric. Press on both sides. Repeat with the other back fabric piece.

5. Place the front fabric on a flat surface, right side facing down. Place one back piece right side up on top of the front piece so that the raw edges line up along the left side and the top and bottom left two-thirds (the bias tape edge will run vertically, slightly off center). Then place the other back fabric piece on top of the pile right side up in the same manner, but with the raw edges aligning on the right side of the front piece. The bias tape edges should overlap 5" running vertically down the middle. Pin around the perimeter of the entire piece.

6. Stitch around the perimeter using a ¼" seam allowance. (I find it much easier to keep the fabrics from shifting if I do this quick basting step. That said, if you are a confident sewer, you could skip this step and start pinning the bias tape in place as written in the next step.)

7. Pin the bias tape around the perimeter of the piece. Use a ⅜" seam allowance to sew the bias tape in place around four sides of the pillow. Press on both sides.

8. Insert the pillow form through the opening on the back, pressing it into the corners, and then smooth out the fabrics that overlap for the opening.

Kitchen Linens

Beautiful vintage kitchen linens and crocheted pot holders await you in every thrift shop, antiques store, and flea market in the land; but due to decades of use, as well as having been used with different foods in particular, they are not always in the greatest condition. The worn ones are my favorites to salvage and rescue— for me, a little stain or rip does not ruin the whole thing. On the contrary, we can use the very best from these overlooked linens to create functional, attractive, one-of-a-kind pieces to enjoy for generations to come. Celebrate their age, showcase their individuality, and use them to make all manner of special somethings!

Photo Cube

When I was a child, my family had a clear acrylic photo cube sitting on the coffee table; it had different funny pictures of family members slipped inside. I searched unsuccessfully to find a similar one, and eventually decided to make it myself. This handmade variation is a terrific project that highlights five of your favorite photos and infuses treasured linens into your home decor as well. Change out the photos as often as you like, and keep the others stored inside the cube to look through now and again.

FINISHED MEASUREMENTS

4" × 4" × 4"

WHAT YOU NEED

- Vintage linens (such as cocktail napkins)
- Balsa wood: (1 piece) 16" × 4" × 36"
- Craft knife
- A small paintbrush
- Wax paper
- Decoupage medium (such as Mod Podge)
- Hot-glue gun
- Five photos sized 3" × 3" (Instagram-type photos would be great for this!)
- Tape

HOW TO MAKE

1. Use a craft knife to cut the balsa wood into 4" squares. (Even though you will only need five for this project, make a few extra just in case the thin wood splits.)
2. Place a piece of wax paper on your work surface to protect it from the adhesive.
3. Paint a thin layer of decoupage medium onto one side of a balsa wood square. Place a piece of your fabric directly on top of the wood, and smooth out any bubbles with your hand. Paint another thin layer of decoupage medium directly on top of the fabric to seal it to the wood. Set aside and allow to dry while you continue to decoupage the rest of the squares with your fabrics. Cut off any excess fabric when completely dry.

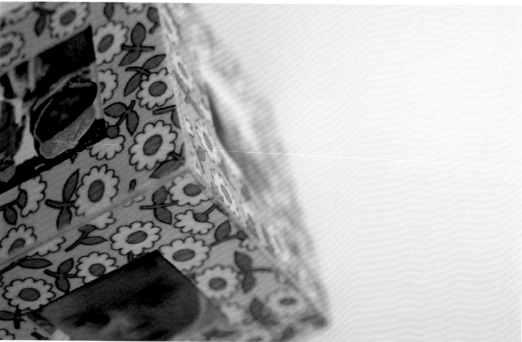

4. Use a craft knife to cut out a 2" square in the center of each piece. Then apply another top coat of decoupage medium to seal the fabric to the balsa wood.

5. Run a thin line of hot glue along one edge of a square to adhere it to an edge of another square at a 90-degree angle. Working one edge at a time, continue to adhere the squares together in the form of a cube (leaving one side of the cube open).

6. Tape your photos inside the frames with right sides facing out.

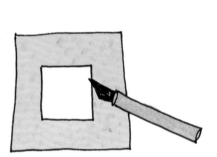 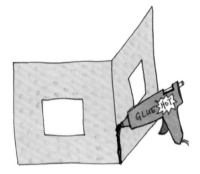

Mini-Project: Photo Mat

It is nice to place larger photos and artwork into proper frames for display. Vintage textiles are a nice way to dress up a simple white mat, and they can provide a sentimental addition to a treasured family photo or artwork when incorporating fabric from someone special.

To Make: Purchase a ready-made cardboard mat sized to fit your desired frame, or use a craft knife to cut out an adequately sized mat from a piece of cardboard. Decoupage your fabric to the mat in the same manner as for the Photo Cube, and allow to dry completely. Working from the reverse side, use a craft knife on a self-healing mat to cut and remove the fabric from the center opening of the photo mat. Tape your photo or artwork to the back of the mat so it faces out, and then insert the mat into your frame for display.

Pretty Pot Holder Zip Pouch

Oftentimes while thrifting or antiquing, you will come across unique crocheted pot holders. I marvel at the handwork that went into making each piece and frequently find them making their way into my shopping basket. In addition to using them as originally intended, you might feature their graphic shapes and pops of color as a decorative grouping in your home, as well as use them as charming accessories. Use a square pot holder to create the bag as shown, or choose two of your favorites to create a pretty little pouch to organize your bits and bobs in your everyday bag. You often can find these crocheted pot holders in interesting shapes. Consider making a smaller version of this pouch using two of your favorites with similar shapes and sizes!

FINISHED MEASUREMENTS

5" × 10"

WHAT YOU NEED

- Vintage cotton crocheted pot holder: (1 piece) 10" × 10"
- Strong thread for hand-sewing in a complementary color (such as 100% cotton quilting thread)
- Fabric for the lining: (2 pieces) 5" × 10"
- 10" zipper (or zipper sized to fit your pot holders)

HOW TO MAKE

1. Fold the potholder in half with the desired side facing out, and pin the two short sides together. Hand-sew the sides together using a backstitch, leaving the top long edge open for the zipper. (See the Stitch Guide on page 121.)
2. Place the lining fabrics right sides together, and pin along one long and both short sides. Sew the three sides of the lining together using a ½" seam allowance. Press on both sides. Turn the top raw edge of the lining fabric over ½" toward its wrong side and press.
3. With the right side of the lining facing inward, place the lining inside the pot holder pouch so their wrong sides are together. Starting at one end of the pouch opening, pin the zipper end in place between the exterior and lining at the

seam. Unzip the zipper, and carefully pin it to each corresponding side of the pouch, sandwiching it between the pot holder and lining fabrics. When you reach the other end of the pouch, tuck the other end of the zipper in between the lining and pot holder before pinning it.

4. Hand-sew the zipper to the pouch using a needle and thread, being careful that you are securing the zipper to the corresponding exterior pot holder as well as the lining fabrics. A backstitch is great for this and will make the zipper extra secure. (See the Stitch Guide on page 121.)

Napkin Hamper

Cloth napkins have a way of giving mealtime that extra bit of specialness. Large ones are great for family meals, and smaller cocktail napkins are perfectly sized to fit into children's lunch boxes. While cloth napkins create no added garbage at the end of the meal, they do have a way of piling up over the course of the week. This cubby is made from two large napkins and hangs on a doorknob near your laundry room so everyone knows where to put their soiled napkins when the table is cleared. Come wash day, toss the napkins, as well as the hamper itself, into the wash for a simple clean up.

FINISHED MEASUREMENTS

Project shown is 16" × 10"

WHAT YOU NEED

- Vintage linen or cotton square napkins in good condition: (2 pieces) 16" × 16"

HOW TO MAKE

Note: Backstitch beginning and end of each line of stitches.

1. Fold one napkin in half on the diagonal, with wrong sides together to create a triangle and press. Sew each of the two shorter sides using a ¼" seam allowance. Topstitch along the fold using a ⅛" seam allowance. Press on both sides. Repeat for the other napkin.

2. Layer the two triangles, and pin together down the long side. Using a ⅛" seam allowance, sew together for 1" starting at one end, and then leave a 4" opening unstitched. Continue to sew together the remainder of the long side. Open it up so it lays flat as a square, and press on both sides.

3. With the opening positioned near the top point of the square, bring point A to point B, and pin the fabrics together. Sew along this short side using a ¼" seam allowance. Then bring point C to point B and sew together as with the other side.

4. Now sew the bottom 6" of the front opening together using a ¼" seam allowance. Press on both sides.

5. Turn inside out and hang over a doorknob through the opening at the top point.

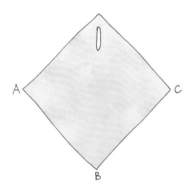 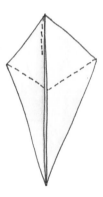

Mini-Project: Handwork as Art

Some smaller linens, such as cocktail napkins and even hankies, feature such lovely hand-stitching that it is worth showcasing their artistry. As a tip of the hat to the hands who created your favorite—if you can choose just one—a simple and lovely project is to mount it onto linen.

To Make: Carefully pin the piece to a larger piece of linen, and then whip stitch or blind stitch on all sides to secure it to the linen foundation piece. (A couple helpful tips: use spray starch on the foundation piece first; and use a large embroidery or quilt hoop to keep your featured piece smooth and free from puckering while stitching.) Hang it on the wall right in the hoop, or wrap the foundation piece around some cardboard and insert it in a frame for display.

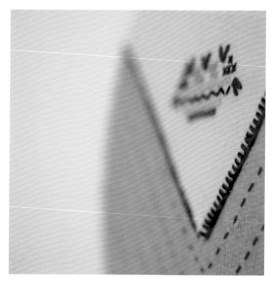 

Tea Towel Picnic Blanket

We keep a special blanket in the trunk of our car for impromptu picnics, when and wherever we feel like it. Vintage tea towels lend their colorful graphics, design elements, and conversation starters to our one-of-a-kind picnic blanket. I love everything about it—the unique vintage tea towels, its antique tablecloth backing, and the quilter's knots my daughters tied with their little hands. (And when not in use, this picnic blanket doubles as the emergency blanket in our family car!) Simple construction combined with sturdy fabrics intended for dining and cleanup creates a functional and decorative showstopper of a blanket you will use again and again.

FINISHED MEASUREMENTS

Project shown 48" × 58" (But you can make whatever size you like.)

WHAT YOU NEED

- 8 vintage tea towels
- One vintage tablecloth or other sturdy cotton fabric for the backing
- Cotton embroidery floss or worsted-weight 100% wool yarn
- Tapestry needle

HOW TO MAKE

Note: Backstitch beginning and end of each line of stitches.

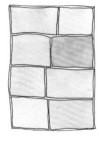

1. Place your tablecloth onto your work surface, and smooth it out. Arrange the tea towels in rows on top of the tablecloth, placing the printing and graphics so there will be something interesting to see and read from every angle. Continue placing tea towels until the tablecloth is covered.

2. Take two adjacent tea towels and sew them together on their corresponding edges using a ¼" seam allowance. Press the seam to one side on the reverse, and then press again on the right side. Continue to work in this manner until the entire patchwork of tea towels is complete. Create two rows, and then sew the two rows together. When finished, press the entire piece on both sides.

3. Place the tea towel patchwork on top of the tablecloth with their right sides together. They are most likely not the same size, but no worries. If the patchwork is too big for the backing, simply trim it to the size of the backing or sew

a strip of complementary fabric or trimming to the backing fabric. And, if the patchwork is too small for the backing, simply trim the backing to size.

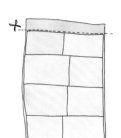

4. Now that the front and back are rightly sized for each other, pin on all four sides. Sew together using a ½" seam allowance, leaving a 10" opening for turning. Press on both sides to set the stitches before turning.

5. Reach through the opening, and turn the blanket right sides out. Press carefully into the corners with a bone folder or chopstick, and then press on both sides. Pin the opening shut, and then topstitch all four sides of the blanket using a ¼" seam allowance. (This also secures the opening closed in the process.) Press on both sides.

6. Use a tapestry needle to sew 10" lengths of thread or yarn ties at each intersection in the patchwork of tea towels. You will pass the thread first from front to back, leaving 4" in front, and then from back to front about ¼" from where the needle went in. Now pass the thread from front to back again close to that first stitch, pull the thread taut, and then finally pass the thread back to the front once again. Make a tight square knot in the tie, and trim the tails to about ½". (Invite your children do the ties, and tell them to make a wish with each knot.)

7. Repeat this step to make ties at each intersecting seam as well as halfway between each, as needed, to hold the front and back of the blanket together.

Dorothy Gale Everyday Tote

There is just something about gingham; it speaks of pure and simple old-fashioned goodness. Gingham evokes memories of picnics, sunshine happy days, and the innocence in Dorothy in The Wizard of Oz. It just makes you smile, you know? Heavier-weight gingham fabrics such as those used in vintage tablecloths provide the inspiring foundation for this terrific tote bag featuring lines of stitching, whipping this way and that. It is a bit retro, a bit modern, and plenty roomy enough to use absolutely every day. (And roomy enough for your little dog, too!)

. . . .

FINISHED MEASUREMENTS

Approximately 13" × 16" with 24" straps

WHAT YOU NEED

- Medium-weight gingham fabric (such as that from a vintage tablecloth): (2 pieces) 10" × 18"
- Medium-weight linen fabric for the bag: (2 pieces) 5" × 18"
- Medium-weight linen fabric for the straps: (2 pieces) 5" × 26"
- Cotton or linen fabric for the lining: (2 pieces) 14" × 18"
- Coordinating thread in the same color as the gingham

HOW TO MAKE

Note: Backstitch beginning and end of each line of stitches.

1. Pin one piece of the gingham fabric to one piece of linen for the bag, putting right sides together and aligning them along the long side. Sew them together along the long side using a ½" seam allowance. Press the seams open on the reverse, and then press again on the right side. Repeat with the other gingham and linen bag pieces.

2. Now add decorative stitching to the bag pieces using the colored thread that coordinates with your gingham. For example, with the right side facing up, top-stitch three lines of stitches spaced ⅛" apart on both sides of the seam (six lines of topstitching in all). Add a series of both vertical and horizontal lines extending from the gingham at the base, and then create a mirror version for the other side of the bag so that they will line up at the base of the bag. (Honestly,

you can do whatever you like, and I am sure it will be lovely!) All that stitching can sometimes stretch the fabric, so when you have finished adding decorative stitching, press both pieces on both sides and check the measurements. If needed, trim to size (14" × 18").

3. Fold the strap pieces in half the entire length of the fabric and press. Use that crease as a guide to fold under both long raw edges toward the center, and bring folded edges together. Press on both sides. You should have two straps measuring about 1¼" × 26" each. Topstitch lines running up and down the length of each strap spaced ⅛" apart. When finished, press on both sides.

4. Place one bag piece right side up on your work surface with the gingham side positioned at the bottom. Center one strap 5" in from either side, and pin it to the bag with the raw ends of the strap extending about 1" above the top edge of the bag and the handle looping down toward the bag and the right side of the strap (with the colored stitches) facing the right side of the bag. Sew the strap to the bag piece using a ¼" seam allowance. Repeat for the other strap and bag piece.

5. Place the two bag pieces right sides together, and pin on both sides and the bottom (leaving the top open). Sew together on those three sides using a ½" seam allowance. Press on both sides.

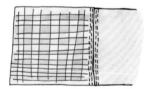

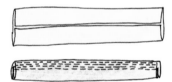

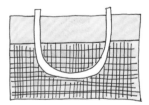

6. Mark a 1¼" square in each of the bottom corners using the stitch lines as a guide, and then cut out the squares. Put your hand inside the bag down at one of the corners, pinch the bottom and side seams together, and pin in place, making sure the seams are pressed to opposite sides to reduce bulk. Repeat for the other corner, and then stitch both bottom corners using a ½" seam allowance to create a boxed bottom for the bag. Press on all sides.

7. Place the two lining pieces right sides together, and pin on both sides and the bottom. Sew together using a ½" seam allowance, leaving a 4" opening at the bottom for turning. Then repeat step 6 to create a boxed bottom in the lining. Press on all sides.

8. Now place the lining right side out inside the bag so that their right sides are together and the straps are nestled in between. Pin together around the entire top edge of the bag, being careful to align the seams. Sew the bag and the lining together using a ½" seam allowance. Press along the entire top seam to set the stitches.

9. Reach inside the bag very carefully through the opening in the lining to turn the bag right side out, gently pulling the straps out as well. Press into the boxed bottom of both the exterior bag and the lining with your hand.

10. Pin the opening in the bottom of the lining closed, and sew it closed using a ¼" seam allowance or sewing by hand using a blind stitch (see the Stitch Guide on page 122).

11. Place the lining inside the bag, and press the entire top edge of the bag with an iron. Topstitch using a ¼" seam allowance to secure the lining to the bag exterior along that top edge, passing over the straps a few extra times to secure them in place.

12. Carefully press the entire bag inside and out with an iron to set all the stitches.

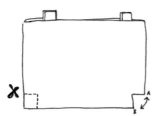

Acknowledgments

I would like to extend my heartfelt thanks to the wonderful people who helped this dream of mine evolve into the very thing you are holding in your hands.

Roost Books, for being a wonderful home for this project and a true pleasure to work with.

Jennifer Urban-Brown, my editor, for her wisdom and kindness while guiding me from proposal to manuscript to book. Lora Zorian, for sharing her technical expertise and design sensibilities to ensure my artwork was just so. Julia Gaviria, for her meticulous finesse with the written word.

Linda Roghaar, my agent, for her enthusiasm, support, and lovely conversations.

The online community I hold dear to my heart, and my devoted blog readers in particular, for support and friendship in art + craft.

Beth, Juliana, Monika, Julie, Kaye, Viviana, Danette, and Pam, for lightness and laughter.

My brother, Rob, for lending his vintage Superbeetle for an impromptu photo shoot before an early summer family dinner. Mom and Dad, for encouraging me to try new things, and for letting me study abroad time and again.

Our dear friends, Desirée + Tony, for insight, style, and camaraderie.

My daughters, Natalie + Sophia, for being my greatest joy and daily inspiration, and for making life sparkle.

And my husband, Patrick. You are the sunshine of my life. xoxo

Stitch Guide

Following are illustrated tutorials of techniques mentioned throughout this book. Included are basic hand-sewing and hand-embroidery stitches, as well as a few bonus patchwork-piecing methods.

BASIC BACKSTITCH

This is a great stitch for outlining and lettering. Working from right to left, and spacing your stitches about ⅛" apart, bring the needle and thread up from back to front through A, down from front to back through B, up from back to front through C, down from front to back through A, up from back to front through D, and so on.

BLANKET STITCH

The blanket stitch is a popular method used for finishing edges of fabrics. Working from left to right on the edge of the fabric, bring your needle and thread up from back to front through A ¼" from the edge of the fabric, and then anchor the stitch by looping it over the edge and bringing it from back to front through A again. Bring the needle through the loop, and then from front to back through B ¼" to the side of A and through the loop at the edge. Pull the stitch tight, aligning it with the edge of the fabric. Continue working stitches in this manner at ¼" intervals along the edge of the fabric.

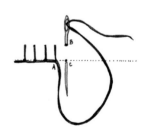

BLIND STITCH

The blind stitch is a hidden stitch that is used for finishing quilts, hems, and anything where you do not wish for the stitches to be seen. Working from right to left, bring the needle and thread from the front through A, running it ¼" through the channel of the turned edge. Bring it up through B while nipping a few strands of the opposite fabric. Continue working at ¼" intervals in this manner.

FRENCH KNOT

French knots are ball-like knots that look terrific in many different types of embroidered projects. Bring the needle and thread up from back to front through A, hold the thread taut in one hand, and wrap the thread around the needle two times. Pull the thread so that the wraps are tight around the needle, and then bring the needle and thread down from front to back right near A (while still holding the thread taut around the needle).

RUNNING STITCH

The running stitch is one of my favorites! It creates a line of dashed stitches, which adds texture and gives an old-timey feel to embroidery. Bring the needle and thread up from back to front, and down from front to back, at ⅛" intervals.

DRESDEN PLATE BLOCK

If you are feeling ambitious and would like to re-create a classic Dresden Block using fabrics of your own choosing, the process is made simple with your sewing machine.

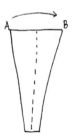    

To Make: Copy and cut out Dresden Plate Block Blade templates (found on page 130). Place a template piece on top of a fabric, and cut out a piece of fabric that is ¼" larger on all sides. Fold the piece in half with wrong sides together, as the illustration shows. Stitch straight across the top end using a ¼" seam allowance. Clip the corner as shown, and turn the piece right side out. Make as many as you wish, and then press all of the blades on both sides. Stitch the blades together along the sides using a ¼" seam allowance. Press the seams to one side on the reverse, and then press again on the right side. When your blades join to create a circle, stitch it to a foundation piece, and use the finished piece to create a pillow or wall art, or assemble several to create an entire quilt.

HEXAGON FLOWERS

If, like me, you have been put off by the mention of "paper piecing" in the past, these simple hexagons are a fun way to break you in with the technique. And they are a terrific way to highlight even the smallest scraps of vintage fabrics. Paper piecing makes a wonderful handwork project to take with you on the go.

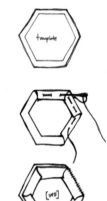

To Make: Copy and cut out Hexagon Templates (found on page 129). Place a template piece on top of a fabric scrap, and cut out a piece of fabric that is ¼" larger on all sides. With the template centered on the wrong side of the fabric, fold over one side and finger press the edge. Use a needle and thread to baste the folded edge through the paper to the fabric and back with a few running stitches. Continue to baste the folded edges in place around the entire piece. Set aside, and make a whole bunch more. Piece the hexagons by stitching the adjacent edges together with right sides facing. When your desired flower is complete, press on both sides with an iron. Carefully remove the basting stitches and template papers, and press again.

HALF-SQUARE TRIANGLES

This is a quick method to create a square of patchwork consisting of two triangles, better known as half-square triangle patchwork.

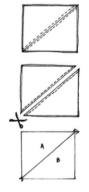

To Make: Pin two squares of fabric right sides together. Use a ruler and pencil to draw a diagonal line from corner to corner. Sew diagonally on both sides of that line using a ¼" seam allowance. Use scissors or a rotary cutter to cut along the penciled line. Press the seams of both pieces to one side on the wrong side, and then press again on the right side. Square up each of your half-square triangles to the desired measurements.

Resources

When looking for treasures such as vintage fabrics and antique cutter quilts, I recommend you shop local. It can be such fun to simply go for a drive and see what you may find. Antiques malls small and large are sprinkled about the countryside to be sure, as are resale and consignment shops. Check the paper for garage and estate sales nearby, and make an afternoon of it! And be sure to search the Internet, as well. There are tremendous resources online to help you find just what you are seeking. Following is a small list of online sources I have used and recommend to get you started as you gather materials to make your treasured heirlooms from timeworn textiles, as mentioned in this book.

Antiques Mall Finder—www.antiquemalls.com
Estate Sale Finder—www.estatesales.net
Flea Market Finder—http://fleamarketfinder.org
Thrift Shop Finder—www.thethriftshopper.com

Fusible Web, Paper-Backed (Wonder Under, HeatnBond)—
readily available at craft, hobby, sewing, and quilt stores

Kraft Paper Cahier Notebooks
  Moleskine Store—www.moleskineus.com
Lavender, Dried Buds
  Mountain Rose Herbs—www.mountainroseherbs.com
Vintage Fabrics
  eBay—www.ebay.com
  Etsy—www.etsy.com
Wooden Discs—readily available at craft or hobby stores
Wool Felt (Thick)
  A Child's Dream Come True—www.achildsdream.com
  Filz Felt—www.filzfelt.com
  Purl Soho—www.purlsoho.com
Wool Stuffing
  Morehouse Farm Merino—www.morehousefarm.com

BOOKS

Embroidery and Needlework

Colton, Virginia, ed. *Complete Guide to Needlework (Reader's Digest)*. New York: Reader's Digest, 1979.

Paulson, Alicia. *Embroidery Companion: Classic Designs for Modern Living*. New York: Potter Craft, 2010.

Patchwork + Simple Sewing

Coleman-Hale, Rashida. *I Love Patchwork: 21 Irresistible Zakka Projects to Sew*. Loveland, Colo.: Interweave Press, 2009.

Karol, Amy. *Bend-the-Rules Sewing: The Essential Guide to a Whole New Way to Sew*. New York: Potter Craft, 2007.

Koseki, Suzuko. *Natural Patchwork: 26 Stylish Projects Inspired by Flowers, Fabric, and Home*. Boston: Roost Books, 2011.

Koseki, Suzuko. *Patchwork Style: 35 Simple Projects for a Cozy and Colorful Life*. Boston: Roost Books, 2009.

Repurposing

Donenfeld, Maya. *Reinvention: Sewing with Rescued Materials*. New York: Wiley, 2012.

Fussell, Tif. *The Suitcase Series Volume 2: Dottie Angel.* Calgary: Uppercase, 2011.

Fussell, Tif, and Rachelle Blondel. *Granny Chic: Crafty Recipes and Inspiration for the Handmade Home by Dottie Angel and Ted & Agnes.* London: Kyle Books, 2013.

Mano, Akiko. *Linen, Wool, Cotton: 25 Simple Projects to Sew with Natural Fabrics.* Boston: Roost Books, 2009.

Okawa, Junko. *Carefree Clothes for Girls.* Boston: Roost Books, 2009.

Soule, Amanda Blake. *Handmade Home: Simple Ways to Repurpose Old Materials into New Family Treasures.* Boston: Roost Books, 2009.

Stocker, Blair. *Wise Craft: Turning Thrift Store Finds, Fabric Scraps, and Natural Objects into Stuff You Love.* Philadelphia: Running Press, 2014.

White, Betz. *Sewing Green: 25 Projects Made with Repurposed & Organic Materials.* New York: STC Craft, 2009.

Vintage Fabrics

Geisel, EllynAnne. *The Kitchen Linens Book: Using, Sharing, and Cherishing the Fabrics of Our Daily Lives.* Kansas City, Mo.: Andrews McMeel Publishing, 2009.

Miller, Susan. *Vintage Feed Sacks: Fabric from the Farm.* Atglen, Pa.: Schiffer Publishing, 2007.

Oikawa, Saeco, ed. *Vintage Fabric from the States: A Visual Introduction to American Vintage Fabrics.* Tokyo: PIE Books, 2009.

Periodicals

Better Homes and Gardens

Cotton Friend (Japan)

Cotton Time (Japan)

Country Living

Flea Market Style

Home Sweet Craft (Japan)

Martha Stewart Living

Mollie Makes (UK)

Stitch

American Institute for Conservation of Historic and Artistic Works—
www.conservation-us.org

Artsy Crafty Babe (Beki Lambert)—www.rebekalambert.com

Dottie Angel (Tif Fussell)—http://dottieangel.blogspot.com

Erleperle (Mette Robl)—http://mette-erleperle.blogspot.com

Flax and Twine (Anne Weil)—www.flaxandtwine.com

Friedas Retro Galerie—http://friedafliegenpilz.blogspot.com

Gretelies—http://gretelies.blogspot.com

Hildas Hem—www.hildashem.se

Hodge Podge Farm (Cal Patch)—http://hodgepodgefarm.net

Kelly Mccaleb—http://kellymccaleb.typepad.com

Kinchi (Mirjam Bos)—http://kinchi.etsy.com

Lotta Jansdotter—www.jansdotter.com

Meet Me at Mikes (Pip Lincolne)—http://meetmeatmikes.com

Pemberlie (Chris Carleton)—http://pemberlie.com

Petits Détails—www.petitsdetails.com

Small Forest (Wendy Hill)—http://smallforestshop.blogspot.com

Smile and Wave (Rachel Denbow)—http://smileandwave.typepad.com

SouleMama (Amanda Soule)—http://soulemama.com

Sparkle Power! (Candace Todd)—http://candacetodd.blogspot.com

Squam Art Workshops—www.squamartworkshops.com

Syko (Kajsa Wikman)—http://syko.typepad.com

Pattern Pieces

HEXAGON TEMPLATES

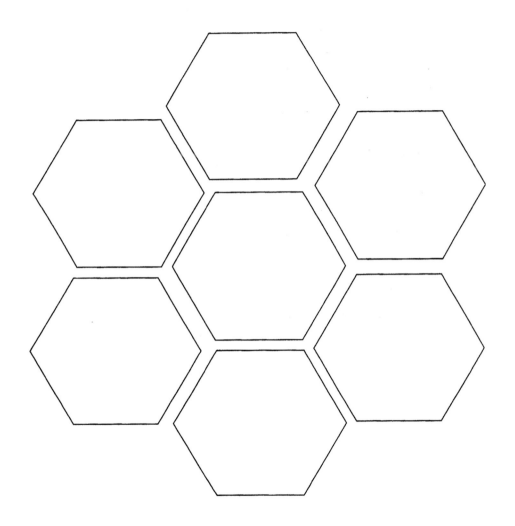

DRESDEN PLATE TEMPLATE

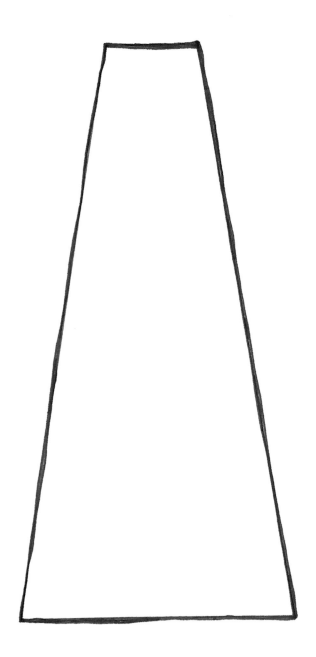

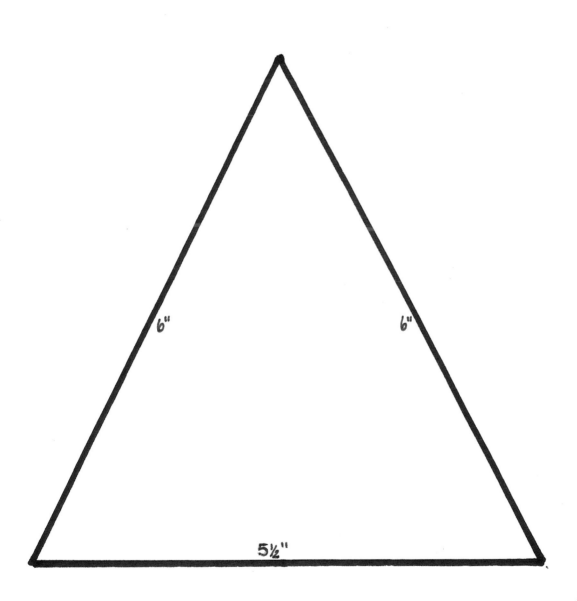

HANAYO BAG TEMPLATE
enlarge by 150%

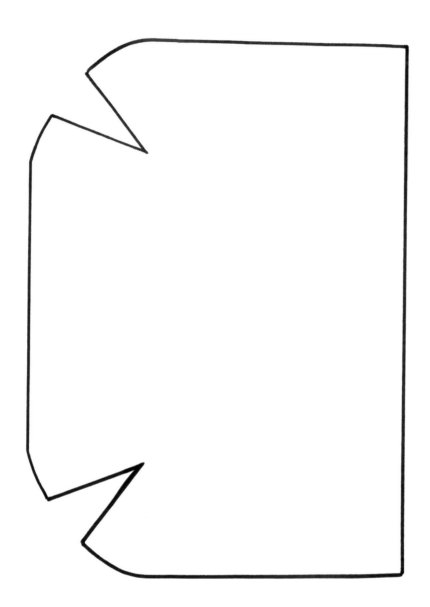

About the Author

Jennifer Casa is a maker of modern heirlooms. She sews, knits, and produces treasured heirlooms from timeworn textiles, combining new + vintage materials in unique handmade pieces that add both function and style to everyday life. Join in making the everyday something special, and connect with her at JCasahand made.com.